A Leak in the Heart

A Leak in the Heart

TALES FROM A WOMAN'S LIFE

FAYE MOSKOWITZ

David R. Godine · Publisher · Boston

First hardcover edition published in 1985,
first softcover edition in 1987 by
David R. Godine, Publisher, Inc.
Horticultural Hall
300 Massachusetts Avenue
Boston, Massachusetts 02115

Some of the essays in this book first appeared in slightly
different form in the following: *The New York Times*
Copyright © 1981; *Woman's Day* Copyright © 1984 CBS
Publication; *The Christian Science Monitor*; "All Things Considered,"
National Public Radio; *Pioneer Women/ Na'Amat*;
The Chronicle of Higher Education Copyright © 1982.
All are reprinted by permission.

Library of Congress Cataloging in Publication Data

Moskowitz, Faye.
A leak in the heart.
1. Moskowitz, Faye—Addresses, essays, lectures.
2. Jews—Michigan—Jackson—Biography—Addresses,
essays, lectures. 3. Jackson
(Mich.)—Biography—Addresses,
essays, lectures. I. Title.
F574.J14M67   1985   977.4'28   [B]   84-48298
ISBN 0-87923-551-9
0-87923-659-0 (pbk.)

Fourth Softcover Printing, 2002
Printed in the United States of America

A Leak in the Heart

I HAD BEEN IN FRANCE MORE THAN A month and, by necessity and design, my graduate school French was slowly improving. Now I could buy my baguette with relative ease, although, I admit, my hands and eyebrows still worked overtime. The francs in my bulging change purse were beginning to look like real money to me, and some days I actually ventured beyond the weather in my conversations with the old man in blue blouse and beret who sold me my *International Herald Tribune*.

One afternoon, I stood in the checkout line at the Prisunic. I had successfully negotiated the minefield of foreign labels and prices mentally translated into dollars. Now I had only the hurdle of the sullen cashier, and I would be safely out on the street. I thought I might even have mastered the art of checking the register while simultaneously stowing my purchases in the shopping bag I had, for once, not forgotten to bring with me.

With confidence, perhaps a little smugness, I approached the cashier. Skillfully, she removed the items from the red plastic basket, rang each one up, and shoved it down the counter. Just as skillfully, I grabbed the purchase and shoved it in my bag, all the while keeping my eyes on the register. The Dim hosiery was on sale and, stubbornly, I wanted that discount.

When the clerk rang up the full price on the stockings, I began my halting "Pardonez-moi," my midwestern accent sickening even me. Behind me, the long line of rush-hour patrons, bound for home, muttered, rustled impatiently. Finally, I managed to get it out. "The price isn't right," I stammered in French. The cashier yawned and scratched under the arms of her pink uniform. If she understood me, her blank expression gave no clue. Meanwhile, the French word for "sale" sunk deeper into the quicksand of my memory.

Sighing audibly, a woman with a squirming child in her arms muttered something to the man next to her. They both laughed. At me? Probably. The cashier shrugged her shoulders, snatched the change purse from my fingers, extracted some francs, and, snapping it shut, pushed the little wallet back into my hands. I was dismissed. Tears stung my eyes, but even more humiliating, my mouth stuck fast, obstinate as a painted-shut window. The purchases of the next customer began to slide down the counter, nudging my bag. I picked up my bundle and fled.

On the street, I leaned my forehead against the cool plate-glass window of a *salon de beauté*. The voices of hurrying pedestrians moiled in my head like dozens of radio stations crackling with static. Here a word came through clearly; there whole phrases faded and were lost. I wept for the familiar landscape of my home but, most of all, I missed the sound of my own language.

.   .   .

Bobbe and I walk downtown to the dime store. To me, she is an enormous woman who swings her great hip against my side with each stride. Three long skips cannot match one of her giant steps. Like hungry jaws, her thick fingers swallow my small hand.

I am a balloon bouncing at the end of a taut string. I wiggle my fingers desperately. My grandmother will not give me back my hand. Why does she hang on to me so tightly? Am I to guard her from the *goyim*, or is *she* protecting *me* from the unfamiliar terrors of my little Michigan town?

We walk: under canopies of elms, sunshades of horse chestnut, maple, and oak, past houses with gabled windows and turrets like birthday hats. A squirrel's fortune of nuts rains down with every wind breath and rolls beneath our feet.

Bobbe looks neither to the left nor to the right. I glance up at her face. Her mouth is caved in like the little dried-apple dolls at the Jackson County Fair. She has left her smile in a water glass on the table next to her bed. Her black wig is slightly tipsy; I can see her gray hair peeking out around it. She does not look like the neat, proper grandmothers of my friends who are not Jewish. I say, "Bobbe, please talk to me in English; this is America."

As we get closer to the stores, we begin to see other people. The women wear flowered silk dresses and soft, stylish hats. Their tiny shoes have pointed toes and little curving heels. My grandmother has an apron over her dress. I wish she would take off her apron and put it in the black shopping bag she carries instead of a purse.

We walk into Kresge's five-and-ten. Bobbe says loudly, "Where is the thread?"

I pretend I do not understand. I say, "Bobbe, please speak English." I hope no one has heard

4

her. Finally, I manage to pry my hand loose.

I watch her warily at the sewing counter. She points to a spool of white thread and asks, "What costs?"

The salesgirl scratches her head with the point of her pencil. "Ten cents."

Bobbe shakes her head. "Too much. I give a nickel."

I call her "grandma." I say, "Grandma, the thread costs ten cents. Give the girl a dime." I pull my grandmother out of the store. She is trying to say something to me in Jewish, but I have put my hands over my burning ears.

Bobbe clutches my hand again in hers. We turn toward home. Then she stops at a curb. She stands with one foot on the sidewalk and the other on the street. She looks straight ahead. Her feet are wide apart. Her wide skirts come down almost to the tops of her heavy black shoes. I do not believe what I see. My grandmother is going to the bathroom in the middle of the street—in broad daylight! I put my head down and walk away from her. Maybe if I cannot see anyone, they will not see me. I have tears in my eyes. I say to my grandmother, in Jewish, "This is America, Bobbe; we do not do that in America."

5

SEPTEMBER IN MICHIGAN: MAJESTIC trees gear up for the last fantastic copper, brown, and yellow blast of Indian summer. Cicadas go bananas with an ever more hysterical warning that fall is here. Then, I remember, was the time for dark plaid dresses and fresh school supplies: the two-drawered pencil boxes that snapped shut over blunt scissors, gum erasers, pen holders, unsharpened yellow pencils and the sharpeners to file them to professional points. But not even the brand-new, triple-decker box of Crayola crayons (including silver, gold, magenta, and chartreuse) could allay my fear of the benighted English teacher who was certain to ask us what we did on our summer vacation.

Peggy Lucille, whose family owned a wood-paneled Ford station wagon, would show picture postcards of their trip out west. Yosemite, Yellowstone National Park: digging a hole deep enough to reach China was easier for me to envision than seeing *my* family on such a trip. Sally's family went up north, Jean's family went down south. Only my underprivileged family stayed home all summer long and did nothing.

Summer mornings, when the sun was not yet fully awake, I often walked with my father to his junkyard near the railroad tracks on the other side of town. On swiveling high stools, we would breakfast at Clara's Diner, at once attracted and repelled by the forbidden scent of bacon buzzing on the griddle like bluebottle flies. We ordered Adam and Eve on a raft and then selected fat doughnuts from under a glass bell or a slice of pie ("We have lemon meringue, apple, and custard today") slipped out of a multishelved glass cabinet that stood on the wooden counter. From a blue speckled enamel pot, Clara poured second cups of coffee into our heavy mugs, wiped the counter with a dingy rag, and asked if it was hot enough for us.

After my father undid the chains and padlocks of the junk shop, I headed for the top of the mile-high pile of books and magazines: *Liberty, Collier's, Saturday Evening Post, Country Gentlemen, Popular Detective, Popular Mechanics.* There were "Big-Little" books with Buck Rogers and Dan Dunn and series books such as Honey Bunch, the Rover Boys, the Hardy Boys, Nancy Drew, and of course, the Bobbsey Twins. My heart pounded for Dan and Buck, forever in danger, but I never really identified with them; they were boys. I longed to be blond and *goyish* like Nancy Drew, whose father was *always* taking her on vacation.

If my eyes gave out, I could sit on a magazine and toboggan to the bottom of the magic mountain. There were the bundles of taffetas, silks, and velvets for doll clothes, stacks of Sunday funnies with "Boots," "Tillie the Toiler," and "Dixie Dugan" cutouts, and items in the Sears and Ward's catalogues on which to squander the inheritance I was sure to get when my real parents finally discovered I had been exchanged at birth. I would have spent my life in the junkyard if it were not for my mother, who was convinced the place crawled with infantile paralysis and TB germs. No hospital floor was scrubbed cleaner than I was once I reached home.

Some days, I would just hang around my block to roller-skate, a skate key swinging officiously from my neck. A hot game of hopscotch required little equipment: a level sidewalk, a round stone to throw, and most important of all, a sharp eye to spot the proper chalky stone with which to draw the squares. A piece of clothesline came in handy, too, for jump rope. Every girl I knew carried dozens of rhymes in her head and could jump for hours if she didn't get the sunstroke my mother was always worried about. "Ice cream, soda water, ginger-ale pop! Tell me the 'nitials of your sweetheart," or "My mother, your mother, lives across the way. Every night they have a fight and this is what they say: Aracka backa soda cracka, aracka backa boo!"

The kids I knew followed our truculent milkman for blocks, begging unsuccessfully for a ride on the running board of his wagon. The iceman, however, was often willing to display not only his tattoos ("All I am or ever hope to be, I owe to my darling mother"), but the knotted muscles dancing in his arms. Sometimes we persuaded him to lift the canvas curtain at the back of his wagon and chip off a sliver of ice with his pick. Then we could suck the icicle until it melted and the cold water ran down to our elbows. Farmers, their carts laden with the morning's harvest, drove by in the early afternoons. My mother would boil corn the moment she bought it, and we would sit on our front porch eating buttered corn and watermelon so ripe it cracked like a pistol when the knife was plunged into it. "Careful," my mother would say. "Don't swallow the seeds. You'll get appendicitis."

There were growing things to be busy with. We picked apart lilacs and sucked the nectar from each tiny floret, gathered shut the trumpets of morning glories and blew into the stem end to make them pop, fashioned hollyhock dolls from a blossom and a bud, wove daisy chains, and stuck dandelions under each other's chins to see "if you like butter." We stole cherries in early July, then risked a bellyache from the tart green apples that followed. Peaches came next, shaken from the tree, and yellow pears on the grass buzzing with wasps. Best of all were the fragrant Concord Blues—the green "eyes" swallowed whole, the dusky skin chewed for its dripping sweetness and then spat out in endless distance contests.

On days when it was too hot to do anything but whine, I went to the PVBLIC LI-BRARY. (For years I worried about how embarrassed the stonecutter must have been when he climbed down from the scaffold and stepped back to admire his handiwork.) There, in the cool, softly lit interior, so like the Christian church I had set foot in once on a dare, I tiptoed past the shushing librarian's curved mahogany desk to the book-lined rooms smelling of library paste and canvas bindings. Little by little, I chipped away at my goal of reading every book in the place. Louisa May Alcott, Bess Streeter Aldrich, Thomas Bailey Aldrich, Gertrude Atherton ... on and on I went, even though my mother assured me I would certainly go blind from all that reading.

Rainy days, I stayed in bed late, watching the fat drops collect on my bedroom window until they were so heavy they ran down the glass in sheets. Later, I could eat my cornflakes and read the back of the cereal box without worrying that I was going to be late for anything. If it happened to be Monday, I might convince my mother that I wouldn't get my arm caught in the wringer, and she would let me lift the sodden clothes out of the Fels-naptha suds, feed them into the clenched lips, and pull them, flat as pancakes, out the other side.

We went to the movies on Saturday afternoons, clutching our quarters: ten cents for admission and fifteen cents for enough jujubes and nonpareils to last us through a double feature, cartoons, *The March of Time*, and previews of coming attractions. Of course there was the serial, too, with its heart-stopping finish, guaranteed to entice you back next week. Outside, after the show, we could barely see for the sun shining on the mica in the sidewalks and the glitter on the placards.

On sunny Sundays, we might drive to a nearby lake fed by water so clear the sun shot through it to dapple the smooth stones on its wrinkled sand floor. We piled into my uncle's Chevy, loaded with picnic baskets, lemonade jugs, towels, and sweaters, and sang popular songs all the way to the lake. "Down in a Meadow with an Itty Bitty Poo," "Who's Afraid of the Big Bad Wolf?," "Playmate, Come Out and Play with Me." My mother, in her bathing dress and yellow coolie straw hat, sat near the edge of the water and kept a sharp watch. We were allowed to go in up to our knees and no further. None of us could swim; the water terrified her. We laughed and splashed. She would step in gingerly and pour water down her front with a cupped hand. In shadowy wooden bathhouses, we pulled off our wet suits and dressed, our clothes suddenly a size too small for our languid, sun-prickled skin.

Threading through the lazy days like a circuit that connected us all was the radio. Up and down the neighborhood we shared the travails and joys of our favorite daytime serial characters: Our Gal Sunday, the Goldbergs, Vic and Sade, Just Plain Bill. The voice of Harry Heilman blared out all over the block, describing, play by play, the fate of our beloved Tigers as they battled in Briggs Stadium. I drew score cards, computed averages, dreamed of the day when I would be lucky enough to *see* a game. Evenings we listened to Jack Benny, Fibber McGee and Molly, George Burns and Gracie Allen.

President Roosevelt's "Fireside Chats" were solemn events; we ringed the radio, and even my little brother had sense enough not to talk. My father would look at the photograph of the president hanging on the living room wall and say, "Roosevelt is a friend to the Jews." One summer night late in June, my whole family gathered to hear the world heavyweight championship fight from Yankee Stadium in New York. Our favorite, Joe Louis, of Detroit, knocked out Max Schmeling in the first round. My father pounded his fist in his palm and said, "Good! To hell with the Nazis." He and my uncle drank a schnapps. I understood it all had something to do with what was happening in the old country, and I was so excited I ran around the block with the other kids, banging two pot lids together.

Some special evenings, we might all walk down to the corner ice-cream parlor and slurp sodas at round tables under whirling wooden propeller fans. Sometimes we just sat on the front porch to cool off. My mother and father would talk quietly

13

about I don't know what, and, safe in their shadow, I would think perhaps I belonged to them after all. Hot nights like that, we carried our pillows downstairs and slept on the living room floor, my mother and father side by side, my brother and I at their feet. So the loosely woven days unraveled with only the Fourth of July fireworks for punctuation. Was it any wonder, then, that when my teacher smiled at us in September and asked the inevitable "What did you do on your summer vacation?," my answer was a shamefaced "Nothing."

PASSOVER? A PIECE OF CAKE NOW, COM-
pared with the days when my grandfather marked
the holiday's beginning by searching for crumbs
of leavened bread with a candle and turkey
feather duster. Today everything from chocolate-
covered matzo to ersatz "bacon" can be purchased kosher for Passover. Years ago, the ritual
search preceded eight days of abstinence from
many foods we considered dietary mainstays.

During the middle of Passover, when we were
permitted to go to school, most Jewish children I
knew shunned the cafeteria and brown-bagged it
with lunches that were virtually interchangeable:
a crumbling piece of buttered matzo, two hard-
boiled eggs with yolks the tarnished green of old
brass candlesticks, and a hunk of sponge cake.
Breaking matzo together gave us a sense of com-

munity, but griping about our restricted diet truly bonded us.

By the time we were both approaching our teens, my cousin Sara, the rabbi's daughter, had begun to question the very foundations of the rituals she practiced so assiduously (and so ostentatiously, if I may say so). I had had my own crisis of faith a year or so earlier when the furtive consumption of a bacon, lettuce, and tomato sandwich at Woolworth's failed to bring forth the expected lightning bolt, so I was ready to share Sara's apostasy.

The spring Sara was thirteen and I twelve, my family came to Detroit for Passover, and I stayed at Sara's house. As usual, the Michigan weather double-crossed us that year. I remember Sara and I went walking in our new spring suits, fat white bobby sox, and the glaring brown-and-white saddle shoes we were under penalty of death not to scuff. Several inches of wet snow had fallen, perversely, the night before, and we hadn't been outdoors five minutes before our teeth were chattering. We didn't even discuss the possibility of covering our recently purchased splendor with last year's winter coats, and we headed toward the drugstore at Twelfth and Pingree, where I, at least, hoped the sight of some neighborhood boys might bring some heat to the situation.

Every couple of blocks, it seemed, we would run into some old woman or other who attended my uncle's synagogue and who, of course, knew Sara. That always happened when we walked together near her home. A two-bit trip to the bakery with her was like taking part in a royal progress, what with all the nodding and bowing. Believe me, Sara took advantage of it, too, holding her head high and acknowledging the stares as imperiously as any princess.

In those days, the Jewish groceries either closed down for the holidays or covered their regular stock and sold only food permitted for Passover. We looked in the shop windows for a while . . . not much to relieve the monotonous displays of matzo boxes stacked in pyramids. Sara skillfully swiped a couple of walnuts from a crate outside a store. I had that feeling I always got when near her: half anticipation, half apprehension; you never knew what she would do next. She was moaning, "Milky Ways, I'd give anything for a Milky Way!"

"Three more days," I said primly. "Three more days, and you can eat Milky Ways until they come out of your ears, and toast and butter, and ice cream and peanut butter sandwiches. . . ." I was getting carried away, but Sara wasn't listening to me.

17

By this time, we were almost at the drugstore. Sara stuck a fifty-cent piece in my hand and said, "You do it. They all know who I am around here." Like a sprinkling of brown sugar, the freckles stood out on her white skin. "Get nine of 'em," she said. I didn't know what she was talking about, and I must have looked like an idiot because she pushed me on the shoulder and said, "Nine Milky Ways, dummy, and hurry up!" I could feel the wet slush coming up through my saddle shoes, and my teeth were knocking together again. Yes, we had been having a theoretical discussion earlier about loss of faith and all that, but as arenas for testing belief, the anonymity of Woolworth's was one thing, and Twelfth Street another.

Up and down the sidewalks, an army of tight-lipped women with black shopping bags marched, each a potential informer. "Sara," I said, "you're really crazy. I'm going back to the house."

"Go on, chicken," said Sara. "I'll do it myself."

So I walked up to the drugstore candy counter and asked for nine Milky Ways. For all the attention paid me by the yawning clerk, I might have been simply buying candy instead of committing a heretical act.

Sara and I carried the white paper bag around for a while, just savoring the latent explosive qualities of its contents. "Good afternoon, Mrs. Rabinowitz," Sara said politely to a woman in bifocals whose gray hair curled out from under an elaborate blond wig. "The old bag," Sara said. "If she had X-ray vision, her eyeballs would fall out on the sidewalk." At that unlikely picture, we burst into nervous laughter and leaned against the side of a building, gasping until our stomachs hurt.

The clock on the white-tiled wall of Katz's Kosher Butcher Shop read 3:45, and Sara said, "We'd better get rid of the evidence." I was still stupid enough to think that having made a symbolic gesture of defiance, Sara would be content to shove the bag of forbidden candy in the nearest trash can and go home. Instead, she pulled me into the dark vestibule of an apartment building over some stores facing Twelfth Street.

The hall reeked of gefilte fish and Roman Cleanser, and I felt sick even before Sara broke a Milky Way in two and said, "Here, we each get four wholes and a half." This was no time to observe the proper amenities of eating Milky Ways: slowly nibbling off the chocolate covering, pulling hunks of nougat with the fingers, and finally allowing the sticky caramel to dissolve on teeth and tongue. Half crouching in the dimly lit hall, we wolfed the bars, hardly taking time to chew, white-faced, hearts pounding.

After the third bar, I said, "Sara, I'm going to puke." Fish and bleach and the cloying sweet made the candy come back bitter in my throat. "I've gotta get some fresh air."

Sara stood barring the glass front door, chewing and gulping. "My gosh," she said. "Here comes Mrs. Litvin. I think she *lives* here."

I said, "Sara, I don't care. My *teeth* ache."

"*Chew*," she hissed at me.

Afterward, we threw the bag and candy wrappers down the apartment's incinerator and made it to the alley behind the building before we started throwing up. I felt the vomiting was punishment from God. If Sara did, she never said so.

MY MOTHER WROTE ME ONE LETTER IN her life. She was in California then, seeking treatment for the disease whose name she was never allowed to utter, as if in some magical way, speaking the illness would confirm it. I found the letter in a dresser drawer the other day, written in the round hand of Americanization school on tissue-thin paper banded at the top with the narrow red edge of gum rubber where it was once attached to a tablet.

March 7, 1947

Dear Faye Chaim and Roger,

How are you kids? I am filling little better. My beck still hurts. Today I was at doctors for a light tritement and Saturday I am going again for a tritement. I hope to god I

*shut fill better. Please write to me. How is
evrething in the house? How does daddy fill.
The weather is her wondufull nice and hot.
I was sitting outside today. Well I have to
say good night. I have to be in bet 9 o'clock
for my health. Take care of daddy.*

your mother

Regart from evrywone.

On the back flap of the envelope, she had written her name, Sophie Stollman, and the street address of the sister with whom she was staying in
Los Angeles. On the last line she had lettered in
Detroit, Mich., her home. Now, older than she
was when she died, I am shattered by that confused address. Loneliness, homesickness, and fear
spill out of those laboriously penciled words, and
the poignant error that was not a mistake, speaks
to me still.

I suppose I realized from the beginning that
my mother's illness was a serious one: I had seen
the fearful loss of symmetry where the breast had
been, the clumsy stitching around it, like that of
a child sewing a doll's dress. I had caught her one
morning weeping in front of the mirror as she
poked at the rubber pad that kept working its way
up to the open collar of her blouse. But I was six-

teen years old and worried enough about keeping my own physical balance. One false step and I might fall off the edge of the world. I was afraid to walk the outer limits of her sickness; I dealt with death the way the rest of my family did . . . by denying it.

I buried myself in books, played the "will-he, won't-he" games of adolescence, worried about the atomic bomb, tried to keep my little brothers from acting like children in a house where the sounds of childhood were no longer appropriate. My father and I clung to each other, but the veil of my mother's illness fell between us, too, and we were silent.

She got worse, and the family began to gather. Covered dishes and pots of food appeared, crammed our refrigerator, molded, were thrown out and replaced by still more food. Visitors came and went, swirling like snowflakes in the downstairs rooms, sitting around the kitchen table drinking tea from glasses, talking, talking. Still, they said nothing, and it seemed to me, sometimes, their silence would awaken the dead.

A time came when my mother's wardrobe was reduced to open-backed hospital gowns; our home was invaded twenty-four hours a day by a succession of starched uniforms and the incessant whisper of white nylon stockings. My mother was terrified by hospitals and refused to go, but still we were forced to trust her to the hands of strangers. She lay, as in a crib, imprisoned by iron bars; her own bed, where she had slept, knees in my father's back so many years, had been taken down to make room for a mattress scarcely wider than a coffin.

Alone for a moment, she called to me one day as I tiptoed past her bedroom. (Perhaps the nurse was downstairs preparing the unfamiliar food on which they kept her alive.) I stood next to her, watched her pluck at a fold in the bedclothes, smooth them, try to make the question casual by the homely gestures. "Faygele," she said, finally, "do you think I will ever get better?"

How could I answer her truthfully, being bound as inextricably as she was by the rules of the complicated deception we were playing out? Perhaps I understood in my heart's core that she was doomed, but I hadn't the permission of knowledge; I could only answer, "Of course, of course," and help to wrap her more tightly alone inside her fear. She never asked me that question again.

A few weeks before my mother died, when the sounds coming from her room began to move beyond speech, an older cousin was given the responsibility of articulating to me the name of her

disease. I remember he took me to an Italian res-
taurant where we stirred the food around on our
plates, and to a movie afterward.

Cordoned off by heavy velvet ropes, we stood
in line under the prisms of rococo chandeliers,
and there, surrounded by people I had never seen
before, I was told the truth, at last. No room to
cry in that glittering lobby, fire spurting from
crystal lamps and mica-sparkled placards. So I
sat, in the darkness of the theater, watching
Johnny Belinda flickering on the screen, the salt
of buttered popcorn swallowed with the salt of
tears.

I was out late with friends the night of my
mother's death. Walking alone up the darkened
street, I saw my house, windows blazing as if for a
party, and I knew what had happened. Word
must have already spread, for on the sidewalk behind me I heard low voices and soft footsteps,
stripped of purpose now, by her surrender.

.   .   .

In my mother's room, the mirrors, according to
the old custom, had been shrouded (so the
mourners would not have to confront their grief,
some say), and damp, chill February fluttered
curtains at the open window. My uncle, in a
heavy jacket, sat next to his sister's bed. He

would watch her until morning. "No, I'm not afraid," I told him. "Let me sit with her a little while."

She lay, hair bound in a white cloth, and I could feel her body, blood and bone under the sheet, pulling away from me, slipping into stone. The memories crowded around me, witnesses to my guilt: the many times I had resented caring for her, the times I had yearned to flee my house when her pain became an intimation of my own mortality.

I remembered, in the bas-relief of shame, the evening I came home from somewhere, to find her leaning on the kitchen sink, washing a stack of dishes I had left undone. "Shut up!" I had shouted when she spoke to me, angered at the robe and slippers, the cane lying on the floor, the medicine bottles, accouterments of a mother too sick to care for her own. Now we were cut off in midsentence. Now I would never be able to tell her how sorry I was for everything.

I still grieve for the words unsaid. Something terrible happens when we stop the mouths of the dying before they are dead. A silence grows up between us then, profounder than the grave. If we force the dying to go speechless, the stone dropped into the well will fall forever before the answering splash is heard.

KRAKOW, THE OLD BOBBE USED TO SAY, was not built in a day. A pity I didn't meet her sooner; I might have spared myself some knocks on the way to growing up. All limp hair and baby fat, I was the kind of girl whose doting parents comfort themselves with, "Wait until she gets to college; by then the boys will have matured enough to appreciate her." In other words, socially, I was a flop.

At twelve, I enviously watched the teenage girls saunter to Central High in their powder-blue and powder-pink angoras, and I dreamed of the time when I would have my very own fuzzy pastel sweaters to keep in the refrigerator at night. By the time I was fourteen, I was smart enough to see that the sweater set (now cashmere instead of angora) would never welcome me, so I joined the Zionist movement instead.

Movement girls wore old World War Two army clothes and no makeup in the time when white bobby sox and Revlon's "Fatal Apple" were standard equipment. We stuck together and snubbed our peers, who belonged, we felt, to the decaying bourgeoisie. I was at first happy in the movement, but two events ultimately convinced me that I wasn't meant for the true collective life.

The people in my Zionist group had a kind of laissez-faire arrangement with kids in other movements to the left of center. Sometimes we attended each other's social gatherings, or we found ourselves thrown together at cultural events such as the premiere of *Fantasia*, where I met my first real boyfriend, Sheldon.

Sheldon told me right off he was a Trotskyist and I told him he had better shut up about that at my house. My Orthodox family, still waiting for the messiah to carry us on his wings to the Holy Land, found my Zionist leanings heresy enough. I could have brought home a Gentile boy and caused less consternation than if I had introduced them to an uncamouflaged Sheldon.

As for me, my reading at the time ran to Rilke and D. H. Lawrence, so I was a little deficient in the political ideology department anyway. I did keep a copy of *Das Kapital* next to my bed, but that was mostly to annoy my parents. I never could get past the first couple of pages.

Sheldon was terribly exciting, it seemed to me. He dressed like a radical with a belted navy blue trench coat he never took off and a heavy briefcase that never left his side. My friends speculated endlessly that he carried a bomb in the case, and we pictured it as in the cartoons, perfectly round and black with a long fuse.

One evening, Sheldon took me to a Socialist Workers party banquet to hear a speech by their candidate for governor of the state of Michigan. I understood, of course, that the race was more symbolic than anything else. The S.W.P. never garnered more than a handful of votes each election, but their slate of nominees for the state administrative offices included a woman and a black. That was pretty heady stuff for 1947, and I was impressed.

There were about thirty-five of us at the gala banquet. We feasted on spaghetti, paper plates piled high with sticking-together strands of pasta topped by a thin orange colored sauce which left a puddle of grease at the bottom of the plate. The salad was even more institutional: cut-up iceberg lettuce, lying limply in another puddle of oil. It was all right, of course. Food is not important in movements. In fact, the worse the food is, the more convinced you are that you truly belong to a movement.

The speeches trailed on through dessert, individual bricks of three-colored ice cream, wrapped in paper. You carefully undid the wrapper and then ate the ice cream from its paper on your spaghetti plate. (Movement people make optimum use of everything.) Bottles of "dago red," served throughout the meal, distinguished the banquet from an ordinary dinner. Since my only previous drinking had been confined to sweet Manishewitz on Jewish holidays, I found the sour wine foreign to my taste, but I tried to be open-minded about it.

We were all expected to help clean up after dinner. I crumpled the sodden paper plates and poured the dregs of the paper cups down a rusty old porcelain sink at the back of the cavernous hall. I felt pretty damn communal about the whole thing until Sheldon grabbed me by the arm.

"What the *hell* are you doing?" he hissed.

I poured another quarter-inch of dago red into the sink and tossed the paper cup into an overflowing metal garbage can.

"What does it look like I'm doing?" I asked smartly.

"Let's get out of here."

He yanked me out of the hall and down the steep stairs so quickly I didn't even have a chance to say goodbye to anyone.

"Idiot, idiot," he kept repeating. "You'll never be anything but middle class."

"What did I *do*?"

"I'll never be able to show my face with those people again," he moaned. "Don't you know you're never supposed to throw anything away that's still useful?" He turned up the collar of his trench coat. "You should have poured the wine back in the bottles."

Me? Pour the wine back into the bottles? Not with *my* mother! When my mother came to America and discovered germs, she experienced a kind of epiphany from which she never quite recovered. Ever afterward, she drove bacteria from her house with the religious fervor of a rabbi exorcising a dybbuk. My mother's floors were of the legendary variety you could eat from. You could, but try it. Once, as a small girl, I tried surreptitiously to retrieve a jawbreaker that had dropped out of my mouth and rolled across one of those chaste floors. Mama, eternally vigilant, gave me a clout that left me disoriented for hours. No, no used wine in old bottles for me.

31

I hung around the Zionist movement for another year or so, dancing the hora, marching in picket lines, singing union songs, and once I even dropped anti-White Paper leaflets from the top floor of Detroit's staid department store, the J. L. Hudson Company. Then, in 1948, the State of Israel was created and I went for a week to a training farm in New Jersey, prepared to educate myself for life on a kibbutz.

The farm at Creamridge was all I had expected: dirty sheets, day-old bread, and uncolored margarine if you wanted a snack. Everyone wore pants and said "Mother!" a lot, especially the girls, and I was told several of the *chaverim* were living together; I felt quite grown-up and intense.

By this time I was fairly experienced in the mores of collective living, pouring back leftover milk after dinner and saving crusts for bread pudding. You wouldn't catch me making the dagored faux pas again. I spent the first day figuring out where to eat and how to find the B.K., the anglicized shorthand for "house of the chair." I also selected an outfit from the communal stacks. Like nuns, we left our outer-world clothing in little baskets that were tucked away somewhere against the day when we might decide to renounce our vocation.

A handsome, incipiently bearded comrade from Pittsburgh offered to show me the farm, mostly given over to the breeding of chickens. The whole scene reminded me of traumatic visits to the kosher slaughterer when I was a kid. I pretty much decided if I had a choice, I'd find a collective in Israel that specialized in vegetable farming.

The next day, I was assigned to the egg-candling detail. Veterans assured me that it beat cleaning coops, so I was content. My Pittsburgh friend led me to a small, damp, evil-smelling room with weeping cinder-block walls and a great electric light bulb hanging from a naked black wire.

"O.K.," he said. "Clean the egg with sandpaper and then hold it up to the light. If you see anything funny, throw it out."

The last thing I wanted to do was show my utter lack of sophistication in the chicken world, so I nodded when he asked, "Do you get it?" He was impatient to take off for the hayloft, where I imagined he anticipated some communal living with a fellow movement member, and I didn't keep him.

"One other thing," he said as he started off. "The dog gets the rejects. Like this . . ." ZAP!

He threw an egg to the dirt floor, and a sleek-

33

looking mongrel with a healthy coat went *shlup*
. . . *shlup*.

Feeling important, useful, *committed*, I orga-
nized myself carefully. To my left were stacks of
eggs in slatted wooden crates. They didn't exactly
look like what came out of the refrigerator at
home. These eggs were brown, and besides they
were covered with bits of straw and chicken
droppings. To my right were crates already half
filled with cleaned chocolate-colored eggs.

Gingerly, I picked up an egg and carefully
sanded away some substance I couldn't even
identify. Then I held the egg to the bare bulb. . . .
It had a spot in it. No mistaking that. ZAP!
Shlup, shlup went the fat dog. I selected another egg. Up to the light. No good. ZAP! *Shlup,
shlup*.

I was ankle-deep in egg shells when my trainer
returned, his arms intricately wound around the
arms of his girl. He surveyed the carnage. The
dog lay in a corner, comatose.

"Boy, did you give me a bum bunch of eggs," I
said as I professionally sanded another egg and
held it to the light. ZAP! On the floor. The dog
didn't move.

"What the *hell* are you doing?"

By this time he had untangled himself from his
girl. I was bewildered.

"But you said . . . if they looked funny . . ."
My voice trailed off. "These all have spots," I
said weakly.

"*Spots!* You cretin! Of course they have spots!
They're all fertilized eggs. Jesus Christ, you are
hopeless."

I NEVER DID GO TO ISRAEL. SOMEHOW
that simple communal life always ended up being
far too complicated for me. I left the movement
when I was eighteen, got married, and, with my
husband, embarked on another kind of communal living. Like many other couples of the time,
we had little to start with but our marriage li-
cense and the G.I. Bill. Housing was scarce in the
post-war pre-building-boom forties, so we moved
into my husband's home with his recently wid-
owed mother, a teenaged brother, and his tiny
hunchbacked grandmother. I was determined
that the lessons I had learned in my movement
days would not be forgotten. There was a right
way to live and, fortunately, I knew what that
was.

My mother-in-law was still in shock from the

loss of her husband and presented no obstacle to my master plan. My brother-in-law, courting a young lady, spent more time at her house than at his own; he was no trouble. My husband, of course, had realized for years how inefficiently his house was run. He saw things my way. The old lady was not so easily dismissed.

It seemed to me that she ran the household from her bedroom, where, propped high on feather pillows, she looked out her doorway across the hall to the bathroom. She guarded that bathroom like some dogged little Yiddish Cerberus, shouting, "Lift up the board," to any hapless male who needed to use the facilities. Daytimes, when the men left the house, Bobbe Frieda could relax her vigil and attend to her other responsibilities. Bobbe, too, I discovered, had a vision of the right way to do things.

She and I both saw that unless our meager income was supplemented or drastic economy measures taken, we were simply not going to be able to pay our bills. She also knew that the economic base of our little commune resided rather shakily in my husband, who still retained enough of his adolescent habits to view getting up in the morning as a matter of choice rather than obligation. She could hardly have avoided hearing, in our cramped quarters, the threats, pleas, and even tears as I struggled to get the breadwinner out of bed and off to college and work. Yes, Bobbe and I agreed on the problem, but when it came to the solution, as my husband said, we each sang our own tune.

One morning, after the men had gone out, I called a meeting of the women. My mother-in-law and the old lady listened as I explained the situation and outlined a few directives: whatever money we earned was to be pooled and kept by my husband in a community purse, or *kupah*, as we had called it in the movement. After paying off the corner grocer, who had been only too happy to keep us in permanent debt by "putting it on the bill," we were to shop solely at cash-and-carry stores. We would begin to plan menus for the week instead of impulse buying every day. Food storage was no longer a problem since the icebox, I reminded them, had been replaced by a refrigerator ten years before.

The old lady interrupted then to say, "*Oy, Gott,*" as if to herself, but I ignored her and went on. We would take advantage of seasonal food bargains, buy day-old baked goods, and can and preserve what we could. All this in the best Department of Agriculture tradition. Between-meal snacks were forbidden except for bread and apple butter. The women looked uneasy at that one, but since I think they both viewed me as a storm that would blow itself out, they said nothing.

The meeting concluded, I went to my room to plan menus. My mother-in-law snuck into the kitchen to make coffee, and Bobbe, an activist like me, went out to solve the problem in her own ways. Like the enterprising little pig in the children's story who was forever outsmarting the wolf, Bobbe was always one step ahead of the junk man. She scavenged the gutters in our neighborhood for pop bottles so she could return them to the grocer for the two cent deposit. Oil-drum trash barrels in back alleys were treasure troves to her. She was so short, I wonder now how she could see inside them, but she did and found plenty, too, to drag to the junk shop, where she let the junk man have her booty for a price.

She didn't look odd to us, but I suppose she must have been a strange sight, scarcely taller than a child, a kerchief knotted at the back of her head, barely covering thin, colorless hair and pendulous earlobes pierced by tiny brown stones. Her body was wrapped, winter and summer, in aprons and sweaters with several pairs of thick cotton stockings wrinkling on her swollen legs.

She kept busy all day as she had almost all her life, buying and selling.

Her favorite scheme, though, was dealing in handkerchiefs. Fagin, had he only known her, would have made her a full partner. There was nothing dishonest in it, you understand. She only dealt in *lost* handkerchiefs, ones that tumbled from an ample bosom, fell out of a handbag, or came out of a back pocket when a gentleman removed his wallet.

Being my mother's child still, I was certain those bits of cloth crawled with TB and polio germs, and I told her so when I discovered what she was doing. She paid no attention, of course, and came home each afternoon, washed the handkerchiefs, pressed them, and sold them to the used clothing store. Later, when for many reasons we became intimate, she told me that the synagogue was her most lucrative haunt. After services, she might haul in four or five sodden hankies dropped by mourners in the women's section who had come to say *kaddish* for their dead.

Some aspects of my five-year plan were eagerly shared. On Thursdays, we took advantage of a deflated Canadian dollar and shopped in Windsor, across the river. Carrying black leather shopping bags, we rode the bus through the long, white-tiled Windsor Tunnel, bringing back eggs, chicken, and produce from the Canadian markets. One day I found a bargain I couldn't resist even though my USDA pamphlets clearly warned against impulse buying. The egg man was offering rancid butter at a ridiculously low price. I thought of a recipe for doughnuts I had been dying to try, and I finally succumbed after a few trips back and forth to the counter. I explained a bit testily to the women when they questioned my purchase that rancid butter was perfectly acceptable for baking.

Back home, we unloaded our groceries while I gathered the ingredients for doughnuts, a surprise for my husband when he came home. My mother-in-law went off to nap, but the old lady sat down to keep me company.

"Faygele," she asked innocently, "what kind of cake are you baking with that spoiled butter?"

"Not a cake, I told you . . . doughnuts, not a cake."

"But you don't bake doughnuts. You fry them, no?"

"Yes," I said, mixing and rolling. "You fry them."

She sat back and folded her arms. "Butter is not good to fry. Butter burns."

I decided to ignore her. Bagels were her orientation, not doughnuts. Besides, I was stuck with three pounds of rancid butter, and I couldn't possibly admit that I had been in error about using it for frying doughnuts. The admission could have jeopardized the entire five-year plan I had in mind for the household.

Bobbe sat quietly, missing nothing as I heated the butter and cut the dough into shape. The kitchen was silent except for the sound of bubbling fat and an occasional *"Oy, Gott"* from the old lady. I dropped the little cylinders, a few at a time, into the pot and held my breath as they puffed, browned, and floated to the surface. Perfect! I carefully turned them over, adjusted the flame and prepared to skim them out. I couldn't believe it. Except that they had cooked faster than I had expected, they looked as if they might have come from the bakery, their plump sides touching in a pasteboard box. I drained the fried cakes on brown paper bags and mixed up another batch of dough. I smiled at the thought of my husband's face when he heard of my bargain and saw what an accomplished cook I was.

I rushed everyone through dinner (my brother-in-law didn't appear) and announced that dessert would be served in the living room. The two women followed me from the kitchen as I carried the plate. Earlier, each had made it clear that she never ate doughnuts. I was on a diet as usual, so we all watched while my husband took a first bite.

"Fantastic," he said. "How did you get the cream filling inside?"

Cream filling? My stomach lurched in misery. They are raw, I thought, as the old lady looked at her fingernails. The butter made them brown too fast. My brother-in-law came in then, breaking what was becoming an uncomfortable silence. He spied the plate of fried cakes.

"Hey," he said, "doughnuts!"

While I sat back in my chair, unable, unwilling, to speak, Bobbe fixed me with glittering eyes and my brother-in-law continued to devour half-cooked fried cakes. My husband finally said, "Take it easy and leave some for someone else."

The plate was almost empty when my brother-in-law left to take a shower, and I waited for the sound of his body collapsing in the tub. Nothing happened, and when he came whistling down the stairs to grab a last doughnut and go out the door, I was thankful we couldn't afford a car; at least no other innocents would be involved when he dropped in his tracks, God knows where.

The remaining doughnuts sat fatly in their plate, a mute reproach to my obstinacy and pride. Like Snow White's poisonous apple, their flawless exterior hid a lethal heart. When I was finally alone in our bedroom with my husband, the burden became too heavy to carry. I confessed my ineptness and took whatever comfort I could from his barely muffled shouts of laughter. I couldn't sleep, of course. It seemed that night as though every other car that passed the busy intersection near our home was an ambulance. It never occurred to me, in my misery, that the ambulance would not reproachfully deposit the victim of my pride at the very threshold of my room.

Onto my stomach, over on my back, up on my side, I twisted and turned to elude the watchbird of my conscience, but there was the slogan fiendishly printed on the inside of my eyelids: THIS IS A WATCHBIRD, WATCHING YOU. I was all the things the watchbird despised: proud and deceitful, bossy and stubborn.

I cried then for a while because I wasn't absolutely certain I wanted to spend my life with the boy who lay sleeping next to me. I cried for my bed at home and for my parents and for my two brothers who had somehow become transformed by distance into Louisa May Alcott siblings. After that, I gave up trying to sleep and decided to sneak into the bathroom to read. Bobbe spotted me when I crept past her door.

"Faygele," she called. "Are you all right? What are you doing up so late?"

Half sitting on the plump pillows to ease her chronic bronchitis, she was reading her prayer book by the light from "next door's" house, an arm's length away.

"Yes, Bobbe," I answered. "I'm O.K. I'm just going to the bathroom."

"I can't sleep either," she said. "Come, keep me company."

She lifted the heavy quilt and patted the bed beside her. I can remember so clearly how gingerly I crawled into the tiny bed, struggling to keep myself at the edge so I would not have to touch the misshapen little bone-bag that was her body. She pulled the blanket up over us both and said, "When you are old, you never want to sleep because there are so many years to sleep soon, anyway."

"I had a dream last night," she told me. "I saw your father-in-law, and I asked, Frank, are you happy where you are? I think he couldn't speak, but he handed me a piece of bread and honey and he motioned for me to eat. You will have a boy," she said firmly, putting her hand on my

45

stomach. "A fat little boy, and he will have Frank's name. That's what the dream meant."

Still keeping a death grip on the edge of the mattress, I started to tell her how the five-year plan made no provision for fat little boys, but I changed my mind. Instead, I let go, rolling to the hollow where our bodies touched, feeling my firm, moist arms, embarrassing in their ripeness, against her powdery, translucent flesh, fearing my chunky body would crush her brittle, twiglike limbs.

Bobbe threw off the covers and took down boxes in her closet. She showed me her wig, a saucy unexpected auburn, part of her dowry when, as a sixteen-year-old, she had married her first husband. From another box, she drew out a thick brown braid glistening with naphthalene. I had the strangest feeling touching the crumbling hair that if I stretched my fingers far enough I could touch, too, the tender young bride who must have cried so bitterly when the women came to shear her heavy hair.

Like me, she had gone to live with her *shviger*, at first. I wanted to ask her if, like me, she had ever wondered just who she was in a household that wasn't really hers. Then I realized she was back in that uncertain position now, at the end of her life. I thought of how she took her scanty meals of rye bread and herring or a few boiled potatoes, perched on the edge of a chair as if she were always ready to give up her place to someone more entitled to it. Yet one thing was obvious to me: from identity crises, she didn't suffer. What experiences had given her a hide as stubborn as black walnut shells? And yes, I admit it. I really wanted to know if she found my charts and directives totally ridiculous.

She must have sensed my tumbled thoughts, for, standing there with the brown braid curled in her palm, she erased the years between us as effortlessly as chalk from a blackboard; she called me, not daughter, but sister. "You don't have to worry; you are like me," she said. "Believe me, Faygele, you are not a *shmatte* as most women are today. No one, you should excuse me, will ever wipe his *tochis* on you. . . ." She shrugged her crooked little shoulders as if to suggest that such strong sentiments required strong language.

What did I care then for the niceties of language? What mattered was that Bobbe didn't see me as the proverbial small kettle that soon boils. She didn't hold against me my watchbird vices. Instead, she was absolutely aware of my efforts to bring order to the household, and what's more, she approved! Such relief. I couldn't wait to admit everything. "About the butter...," I blurted.

She waved her hand at me. "Forget that *narrishkeit*. Remember, Krakow—"

"I know, I know," I interrupted. "It wasn't built in a day." What a beautiful bloodless coup, and it was all over before I realized that *I* was the power deposed.

Back in bed, we talked together for hours, and when my brother-in-law, very much alive, came home and tiptoed to the bathroom, we both whispered in unison, "Lift up the board," and then fell back on the pillows giggling like schoolgirls.

I went downstairs and made toast, and we drank tea with cherry preserves and slices of lemon, eating the thick jam from the bottom of the glasses with long beaten-silver spoons.

EDDY FINEGOOD, WHERE ARE YOU NOW? The penciled scrawl is as faded as my memory of your freckled face, but this much I know: no epic poem in a grad-school seminar ever received a closer reading than the verse you so casually scribbled in my seventh-grade autograph book. "The ocean is wide; / the sea is level. / Come to my arms, / you little devil!"

Betty Sisk, Shirley Mintz, how did your lives turn out? Your names sit on the line marked, "Favorite Friends," at the front of the postcard-sized album with CLASS AUTOGRAPHS gold-stamped on the cover. The year is 1943 and *How Green Was My Valley* is my favorite book, "Pistol Packin' Mama," my favorite song.

Autograph albums were part of the spring ritual when I was growing up. In February, after the stock girl at Kresge's took down the Valentine displays, she piled the little books in the stationery department. With the same inner calendar that told us the appropriate day to begin tossing the first jackstone or baseball, we all knew when to tuck the new albums in our bookbags. Overnight, like dandelions, they popped up everywhere.

Bright sunshine bounces off a shiny crust of snow and filters through tall, newly washed schoolroom windows. Two more weeks till Easter vacation. Deftly we exchange autograph books under wooden desks grown too small to contain our longing to escape.

"Favorite Teacher," Miss Bartlett, raps the blackboard with a bit of chalk. I open a pastel-pink page of Betty Karazan's book and, tremulous with adolescent sentiment, write, "When twilight pulls the curtain back, / and pins it with a star, / don't forget you have a friend / no matter where you are."

How fashions change. What teenager today would bid for immortality with Judy Whipple's entry in my book: "You may have a friend, / you may have a lover, / but don't forget, / your best friend is your mother."

Still, there is a kind of timeless, bare-bones spareness to this terse summary of man's span on earth: "Life is like a deck of cards: when you're a kid, It's jacks; when you're in love, it's hearts; when you're engaged, it's diamonds; when you're married, it's clubs, and when you're dead, it's spades."

Then there are the rhymes that deal with the age-old problem, How does a good man (or woman) live? Nancy Dickinson, the minister's daughter, caught us all up short with this one: "Your future lies before you, / like a carpet of snow. / Be careful how you tread it, / as every step will show."

Perhaps autograph books have gone the way of nickel candy bars and movie star photos on the lids of Dixie cups. In the high school where I teach, yearbooks inscribed with one-liners and cryptic allusions to past exploits are the fashion. I think "Hey, foxy lady" is perfectly fine, but it will never have the bite of this final entry in my autograph book: "When you get married and live by the river, / send me a piece of your old man's liver."

Tommy drowned early in summer when we teachers and his fellow students were still throwing off the school year like our heavy winter overcoats. The Potomac swollen with rain, three boys on an outing, a sudden impulse to try the water, and he was gone. "He never even took his shoes off," we told each other over and over, as if that homely fact could somehow shrink the horror to scale.

There is something disorderly about the death of a young person. In a universe disturbed by so much over which we have no control, an untimely tragedy rattles the teeth of our already shaken confidence. We want to domesticate death, fight it on our own turf, in familiar rooms with shades drawn evenly, top sheets turned back, and a circle of hushed voices closing in. What to do with this unseemliness of superfluous shoes and cries of terror for the final word?

An attic of my childhood: up steep stairs and on the naked landing, stale sunshine trapped in the scent of naphthalene. Here are trunks of winter woolens, tissue-layered, a mandolin with a broken string, a tangle of wire coat hangers, and over all, mouse droppings like scattered caraway seeds. Far under the eaves, the heart-shaped candy box lies, tied with a satin bow. I slip off the ribbon and the photographs slide out, a dozen of them, each in a gray folder, identical, the baby smiling in a highchair, her features ones I know, but I am certain I have never seen her before.

Downstairs, the July heat is almost bearable after the stifling attic. I find my mother in the kitchen, where I expect her to be. I tell her of the baby in the photos, and the look on her face is one I do not understand, almost as if I have caught her in a forbidden act, a look at once sly and guilty, too.

"Go away," she tells me. "Leave me alone."

But these are the wrong words for me. I poke at her and push at her. "Come on," I say. "Tell me who the baby is."

Finally, she bursts out at me, "It's no one!"

How can so many pictures of someone be no

one? I'm on to something now and zero in on her as only a child can do, intuitively knowing the way to the heart's core. "Who is it? Tell me!"

My mother's face is crumpling; she stands at the sink with her hands twisting her apron, crying, "It's your sister, your sister who died. Now go away and let me be."

Such a mixture of emotions to deal with. I had thought myself the first child, the only daughter, and now *this* thunderbolt. Most difficult of all to understand was my mother's grief. She had me, after all, and the other girl had only lived for five years. I heard other details later, because I couldn't let it go. I probed. I learned the name of her affliction. A leak in the heart, they called it; she had been born with it. I heard how precocious she had been. "As though she knew her time was short," my grandmother whispered, one eye on my mother for fear she would hear. An aunt told me how my parents never went back to the apartment where the child had died, had left it all, food in the cupboards, sheets on the beds, had turned the key and walked out.

I was ten years old when I first learned of my sister's existence. What puzzled me most was the depth of sorrow engendered by such a slim life span. I felt my mother's anguish was inexplicable, couldn't fathom why every visible trace of the child had been removed as though the clotting of pain was so fragile, that the merest shudder could set it to bleeding again.

And I didn't understand for years until I had my own baby and saw in that moist bundle of flesh and bone my own freedom and feelings, bound now by inextricable knots that could only be cut but never loosened. Five years, indeed, when each hour that passed rang myriad changes on the flicker of an eyelid, the crack of a smile. A friend wept at her mother's death and would not be consoled. "I'll never allow myself to love anyone like that again," she said, but the two curly-headed girls who sat, stunned to silence by their mother's tears, had already made her words meaningless. . . .

My father married a refugee from the Holocaust soon after my mother died. Left with two small children, he needed someone to care for them. Even my mother's sisters approved his choice. It was a good deed to marry such a woman, one who had "lost" two sons in the death camps. ("Lost," as though she had carelessly misplaced the boys somewhere and might one day remember where she had left them.) "She's been through so much," one aunt told me. "She'll be grateful for anything; she'll be good to your brothers. She lost sons, after all."

So one blistering August day, when even the bluebottles were too languid to buzz, I heard the woman shout at my six-year-old brother, and the words were ripped out of her like so many pieces of flesh, "Why do you live, and my sons are in the ground?" I told that story everywhere in my family, spitting out my own loss and jealousy with every terrible syllable. "Wicked woman," I said to all the sympathetic ears. "What can you expect?" they replied. "Those who survived what *they* saw are animals."

The refugee woman is dead and my father, too, but I still ask her forgiveness whenever I think of that summer day. Out of the unspeakable depths of her loss, the words were wrenched. My brother was there and was splattered by them, but he was not the target. How could we all have so misread her anguish? As if children were interchangeable and one could take the place of another. . . .

Tommy, we file into the rose-lit church: your mother, father, sister, brother, aunts, uncles, friends of your family, and friends from your school, group after group. The girls wear flowing dresses, the boys walk stiffly in their graduation suits, solemn, shaken, most tasting death for the first time. We celebrate your brief life with the old words, share memories we will carry home with us. And then we walk, blinking, into the summer sunshine to hold fast to one another for a little while. Only your young voice is missing from this concord. We file past your parents, blurting out our measured phrases. Onlookers, we stand at the periphery of grief. Life, they tell us, must go on, and it does. But for your parents are left the endless days diminished by your absence, the taste of ashes now forever in their mouths.

I GET THE BLUES AT CHRISTMAS LIKE A lot of other people, but I don't need analysis to find the roots of my depression. Somehow the concept of separation of church and state hadn't trickled down yet to Jackson, Michigan, when I was raised there in the late thirties and early forties. At any rate, Christmas was a miserable time for a Jewish child in those days, and I still recall the feeling.

The pressure would begin in late November, after the new clothes for Yom Kippur and Rosh Hashanah, after the begging on Halloween, after the kosher turkey for Thanksgiving. One day Miss Lukens would strip the bulletin board of its brown-and-black gobblers and black-and-white pilgrims with their axes. Stacks of red-and-green construction paper jammed the supply cabinet, and I knew I was in for it.

Oh, we had Hanukkah, of course: great plat-
ters of steaming potato pancakes, and dreidels,
and all the cousins lining up by age so the uncles
could dole out quarters and half dollars and even
dollars, maybe, to the older kids; but how could a
homely *latke* compete with mince pie and plum
pudding? I can remember the Christmas prepara-
tions so clearly and can feel, even now, my Gentile friends bubbling like seltzer water as the days
were ticked off on the Advent calendar that hung
behind Miss Lukens's desk.

On the first school day in December we spread
back numbers of *The Citizen Patriot* on our
desks while whoever was Miss Lukens's current
favorite doled out blobs of delicious smelling
white paste, scooped from a large jar with a
wooden tongue depressor or Dixie cup spoon.
We smeared the cool, smooth paste on strips of
red or green paper, formed strips into rings, then
slipped rings into rings until each of us trailed a
paper chain onto the floor.

It was on a paper-chain day in Miss Lukens's
class that I began to have my troubles with
Christmas. There I was, threading a green strip
through a red ring when Peggy Lucille Harsch
popped a glob of paste into her mouth and whispered, "You killed our Lord."

"No, I didn't," I answered automatically.

59

What child admits to any accusation the first time? But if my enthusiasm wasn't dampened already, that did it. I didn't know what she was talking about, but I was sure she was probably right.

The days passed, clean snow fell on soiled slush, thawed a little, and then froze into treacherous ruts. Stores stayed open late and folks grumbled that shopkeepers were starting Christmas earlier than ever. Some nights my parents and I walked downtown after dark, snowflakes whirling like moths in the street lamps' halos and the packed ice hard as diamonds under our feet. In the town square, a crèche appeared with a naked baby Jesus stretching out his little wooden arms. Though I didn't know if he was "Our Lord" or not, I suspected he was, and I felt guilty as anything.

Outside the shops, members of the Salvation Army stamped their feet and rang their bells energetically to keep the circulation going. I mistook their red uniforms for Santa Claus outfits and was more confused than ever when my mother dropped a dime into one of the kettles. If we didn't celebrate Christmas, then why were we giving money to Santa Claus? Maybe she felt guilty too.

In Kresge's five-and-ten, coat unbuttoned, thighs jumping with the transition from ax-blade cold to down-quilt warmth, I headed for the music department to listen to my ideal, the yellow-bobbed pianist, bang out the arrangements of sheet music handed to her by prospective customers. Even here, I was troubled. How could I grow up to be a piano player at Kresge's if I would have to play carols at Christmas?

Overnight, twinkling decorations sprang up like great jeweled mushrooms: here a Santa climbed a chimney, there a front door was festooned with greens. I dreaded going home to my house, naked as an angleworm in all that glitter. More than that, I hated going to school, where even Miss Lukens had to concede that her students were too keyed up to learn anything that wasn't sugar-coated with Christmas.

One day she announced we were each to bring in our favorite psalms to write out on the Christmas cards we were making. The stomach-ache, part of my digestive system by then, intensified. OK, I give up, I told myself. I'll bring in my favorite psalm, but what's a psalm? My mother was no help. "Sahm?" she said in Jewish. "Sahm is poison." I was ashamed to ask Ruth Mary, my best friend, and though I was already

61

old enough to use a dictionary, hours of research yielded no "som" or "sam" or any other variant I could think up.

We wrote letters to Santa Claus. What was I to do—write to Judah Maccabee? I crossed my fingers and wrote to Santa. Handmade Christmas presents were not a sin, I told myself, making up the rules as I went along. I would pretend they were Hanukkah gifts even if we didn't exchange gifts at home. So I sewed pen wipers for my dad and found a snowman in a magazine to decorate the holders for kitchen matches that were the gifts for our mothers. The Christmas tree in our classroom grew more beautiful every day, draped with strung popcorn, cranberries, and our paper chains. To me, it was like Snow White's fatal apple, more attractive than I could admit, but evil nevertheless.

When Miss Lukens read us the story of Christmas, my confusion was complete. If Jesus was a Jewish baby, like my brother, for instance, then what was all the trouble about? Why couldn't I celebrate his birthday the way my friends did? Still, I knew there was a catch somewhere, a piece of the puzzle missing that no one would help me find. Then Miss Lukens chose me to be a class representative in the choral group that was to sing carols outside the door of every classroom in the school.

I went home that afternoon and told my mother I felt sick. She put her lips to my forehead and said, "You have no fever. What's the matter with you?" What was the point of telling her my troubles? The only time she had ever come to school was to register me for kindergarten, and then she had answered, "Faygie," when the teacher asked my name, so that even now in third grade I was still called Peggy, the closest match my kindergarten teacher had been able to achieve. The worst of it was I *wanted* to sing the carols; they were the loveliest songs I had ever heard. I took to my bed, hid under the comforter, and refused to go to school.

No candy scent of cocoa, no image of oatmeal swimming in butter and cream, could budge me from my self-imposed exile. My father sat on the edge of the bed in his work clothes, late for the shop, I knew, to give me what comfort he could. By Sunday, my parents were ready to call in Dr. Ludwig, a ceremony usually reserved for the terminally ill. I broke down then and blurted it all out—the guilt, the envy, the anger—and my parents talked to me for hours, gently dealing with one more problem brought on by living outside the Jewish ghetto. In the end, my father softened and told me, "Sing the Christmas songs, but don't say Jesus' name." And so I stood outside the classrooms, my voice blending with that of my friends in the glorious old carols, careful always to omit any forbidden words.

Decades later, I still feel left out at Christmas, but I sing the carols anyway. You might recognize me if you ever heard me. I'm the one who sings, "La-la, the la-la is born."

MY MOTHER CAME TO AMERICA IN THE
twenties in the last of the hopeful waves of immi-
grants. If she ever felt oppressed in her role as a
female, she never communicated it to me. I think
she was far too busy adapting to the ways of her
adopted country to bother with any such ideas.

When I was a child, the mothers of my friends,
like my own mother, stayed home and kept
house. It was hard enough for men to find work
during the Depression. Married women coped
with their husband's shrunken paychecks—or
often no paycheck at all. They put up and let
down pant cuffs and hems until the material fell
apart, stretched the stew until finding the meat
became a game, and sent us to school so well-
scrubbed we squeaked.

No matter how little we had, my mother refused to allow us to consider ourselves in want. I

remember vividly a visit to an aunt's house when I was about five years old. We all sat in the summer kitchen while my mother and her sister chattered endlessly about things that didn't interest me, and I whined and whined, complaining that I was hungry. I couldn't understand why I was offered nothing to eat or why my mother kept motioning me to be quiet. Finally my aunt said, "Sweetheart, how about some bread and milk?"

By this time I really was hungry, and angry too, and I shouted, "Only poor people eat bread and milk."

I'll never forget my mother's face and how fiercely she said to me, "Don't you ever call us poor. We are not poor. Only people who have no hope are poor."

No, my mother would not consider us poor. Wasn't this the Promised Land? In spite of everything, she would make certain the promise was kept. She perceived America as a land where both men and women were capable of unlimited goals. Barriers were everywhere for her, yet she always found a way, if not through them, then around them.

Even though she was having her own crisis of faith, she doggedly insisted that I be proud of my religion in a little town where to profess my Judaism was to mark myself as different from everybody else. At a time in my life when I would have sold my soul in exchange for being 'Piscopalian like my friend Eileen, my mother coaxed me into carrying a box of matzo to school so I could give my classmates an explanation of Passover.

The year I was in sixth grade, one of my teachers decided to put together a school program on the concept of "America as the Melting Pot." She pounced on me eagerly, of course. "Won't you contribute something to the program?" she asked. My stomach lurched in misery. I didn't want to be different, no matter what my mother believed.

I received no sympathy at home. My mother stared at me incredulously when I told her of my reluctance to be singled out. "For five thousand years the Jews have been persecuted because of their faith, and you want to hide your heritage," she scolded. "Go to school and sing them Hatikvoh and be proud of what you are."

"Mama," I said. "What if I sing off key? You know what happens when I get nervous."

She looked at me for a long moment and then she laughed. "How many people in your school know the Hebrew National Anthem?"

"No one," I said.

Triumphantly she pushed the bangs off my worried forehead. "Then who will know if you sing off key?"

Amateur psychology it certainly was, but it worked. Some weeks later, fortified by my mother's advice, I stood in the little assembly room of the T. A. Wilson School while my heart stopped thumping long enough for me to hear the stirring anthem—absolutely on key—ring out over the heads of my schoolmates sitting cross-legged on the floor to their mothers sitting behind them on wooden folding chairs. But my mother, hands clasped in her lap, eyes shining, was the only person I saw.

My mother died in 1948 without ever having seen a television set. My daughter, who was born two years later, watched men walk on the moon while she brushed her teeth one morning. If she has difficulty conceiving of my mother's world, how could my mother ever have conceived of hers?

Yet my mother's life provides me with a good road map into the next generation, if for no other reason than that the detours and dead ends are marked for me. She taught me to hold America to its promise. She had great expectations and no intention of letting her adopted country off the hook. But she also taught me what any Jewish mother knows: a country, just like a child, needs a shove in the right direction sometimes.

MY FATHER'S FATHER WAS A HASID. WHEN he died, he was wrapped in a winding sheet and placed on the front-room floor of his two-family flat in Detroit. His feet pointed east, toward Israel.

As the slow-moving chain of automobiles wound its way to the cemetery the next day, it coiled past his house for the last time. The two-families on Hazelwood were set on narrow lots, each with a few square feet of ground in front. Monopolizing the grandparents' yard was a strange, lumpy tree whose name I didn't know. Every fall, Zayde cut back all the branches, and early each spring, I was sure it was dead, but it wasn't. That was forty years ago.

Then one spring I went to France for the first time, and everywhere I saw plane trees, lining the avenues like endless rows of clenched arthritic fists. Instantly, I flew in memory back through the years to Hazelwood, back to the plane tree knobbily dominating the diminutive patch of nongrass and back to my grandfather, reaching with stiff, yellow toes to a Holy Land he had known only through his prayer book.

Here is the germ of all this: some time ago a student gave me a book to read called *Stranger in a Strange Land*. I was teaching at a university then, and I asked my students about the title. I knew it was a phrase I had seen somewhere before. It's probably from the record by Leon Russell, they told me, "Stranger in a Strange Land." So I listened to the song, and said, "No, wait, it's Camus's *The Stranger* I'm thinking of," but still I felt a clawing at the edges of my memory.

I remembered a folk song I sang to my children when they were small. It told of a lonely Englishman far from home. He is courted by an Indian princess who tells him sympathetically, "You be a stranger in a strange land." One day when I wasn't even thinking about it, I tripped over the phrase in a book I was reading. Yes, I thought, and there's more, surely; and there was. I found my Bible and searched through Ruth, and it wasn't there. In Exodus, I rediscovered it, and I was content for the moment, and then the memory chain began to slip again. . . .

When I was five, we moved from Detroit to Jackson, a little Michigan town of 60,000 inhabitants. The country was in the depths of the Depression; my father thought he might find work there. I remember the Depression as a time when men sat around all day on front porches playing poker for toothpicks. At night, the women complained that the burning porch lights ran up the electric bills, so then we all sat around in the dark and slapped at mosquitoes and just talked. That was Detroit.

There were few Jews in Jackson, and my parents spoke little English. My father had no one to play cards with. We often sat in the kitchen around a red-and-white porcelain-topped table, and we drank hot tea from tall glasses, winter and summer.

My family didn't own any books, but the *Jewish Daily Forward* came in the mail each morning, and I learned to read Yiddish from it. English came on cereal boxes and Bon Ami cans. (I had been reading for many years, though, before I cracked the cipher "Reg. U.S. Pat. Off.") Mondays brought the *Forward*'s Sunday supplement, a rotogravure section printed in rich brown ink. Under the photographs of President Roosevelt, Herbert Hoover, Franco, Mussolini, and Jean Harlow were captions in both Yiddish and

English. I slowly began to make my language connections.

One night when I was about seven, a salesman came to our door. He was desperate; we were lonely. He must have talked his way inside. I recall a stiff new briefcase from which he slipped a large book bound in a pebbly, pale blue material. "Here, sister," he said. "Read this." And so I stumbled through a page, sliding my right index finger under each word as I had been taught in school, my cheeks burning, the sound of my own voice bouncing in my ears.

Of course, my parents couldn't afford that set of encyclopedias, but, convinced by the salesman that my education would never be complete without it, they bought it, and for the next thirty-six months, Elmer, the salesman, became a regular visitor, collecting the painfully put-together dollar a week. I knew little of that.

By the time Elmer marked "Paid in full" in our receipt book, I had worked my way from Volume 1 (A) through Volume 19 (XYZ). It wasn't until I read James Joyce and learned his concept of epiphany that I found a name for what happened to me when I opened that Volume 1 and puzzled out the first entry. *Aa* it was. I can visualize it yet with its crude drawing to illustrate that the Roman letter A came from the Phoenician

73

letter called *aleph*, the word for ox. *Aleph*, the first letter in the Hebrew alphabet, also means ox. There at last was a way to link the *aleph* of my Jewishness to the *A* of my English language, and the land slowly began to be more familiar and the stranger to feel less strange.

So there is nothing new under the sun. I accept that. That is my challenge. There is beauty enough and ugliness enough and love enough and hate enough for any one of us to select from and shape our own absolutely personal combinations. But this shaping must be a conscious thing: a reaching back and forward for those details that create pattern and form and motif in a life. To see living as connection is to bevel the rough edges, miter the corners, blur the divisions so that time becomes a chain of always accessible segments, not fragments, of knowledge and experience.

I believe in the power of a knobby plane tree to carry me backward to the Holy Land; in the power of a book title to write an essay; in the power of *A* and *Aleph* to make me—in some sense—no longer a sojourner, but a native bound, here, then, now, and forever in the connecting chains that set us free.

THE NEW CARRIAGE WAS WOVEN OF wicker: rich brown strands twisted and plaited into rococo curlicues curved like sea waves. Inside, my infant brother lay, a prince amid satin cushions and hand-crocheted coverlets, each tiny feature softened by the gauze mosquito net covering the buggy. My mother's pride was contagious. As we strolled down the sidewalk together, her one hand steering the buggy, the other clasped firmly in mine, the tips of my earlobes bloomed with self-conscious pleasure.

After my mother had bumped the carriage up our front steps, she usually parked it in the front hall. Perhaps Indian summer promised another day of sunshine; perhaps she meant to ask my father to bring it in when he came home from work. For whatever forgotten reason, that particular time, the buggy remained overnight on the porch.

The next morning, in the middle of the street, we found what was left of the beautiful carriage. For half a block, silk and wool, gauze and batiste lay in forlorn shreds. My mother's tearful bewilderment, my father's impotent rage: these are my first memories of Halloween.

At five, I left the mini-ghetto of my home for kindergarten, and for a while I decided Halloween had suffered a bad rap. I even managed halfway to convince my immigrant parents that October 31 was not the annual equivalent of a Cossack raid, but a benign holiday dedicated to the pleasure of children.

For years after that, my mother dutifully took me to Kresge's and waited while I pawed through a gay profusion of sleazy rayon costumes and leered at her through countless cheesecloth masks. With a martyr's patience, she let me lean my forehead against the glass bins of the candy counter and ponder the relative merits of nonpareils and chocolate-covered cherries, peanut clusters and taffy kisses. We always bought too much. People with smashed wicker buggies to remember don't risk running out of sweets on Halloween night.

When I was still quite small, my father, forever

muttering, *"Goyishe mishegoss,"* would accompany me on my costumed forays for Halloween goodies. Hand in hand, we would walk the uphill, downhill sidewalks where cement sometimes stood straight up to meet the stubborn contours of the land. We sauntered past horse chestnuts, elms, and maples to wonderful old houses with high bay windows behind which sleeping beauties might prick their fingers. At door after door, as the torn pillowcase grew heavy with sweets, my father stood by protectively while I gathered my courage and stuttered through my mask, "Help the poor!"

By the time I was nine, I was old enough to disdain mass-produced Snow White costumes from the dime store and sophisticated enough to be embarrassed by the candy-counter chocolates our family offered on Halloween night. I raided the rag bag and fashioned my own costume. And as I sewed I nagged my mother. Why, I wanted to know, did store-bought candy taste of mothballs, and why, for heaven's sake, couldn't she learn to bake something besides sponge cake? Mrs. Teetens, next door, I pointed out, poured cider and handed out crisp, homemade doughnuts, while my best friend Eileen's mother offered the most delicious confection I had ever tasted: a new recipe called Toll House cookies.

"Big shot," my mother would sniff. "If sponge cake isn't good enough for you, go find another house to live."

In costumes of our own design, my friends and I roamed the streets in gangs—pirates with wooden swords and burnt cork mustaches, tramps sporting legitimately smudged faces, female impersonators with shifting rayon-stocking-stuffed bosoms, ghosts draped in discarded bedsheets, and princesses from every conceivable kingdom on earth.

Trading intelligence with other masqueraders, we ran to High Street, where the caramel-apple lady lived, or over to Fourth Street for the cellophane-wrapped popcorn balls. I think we all felt there was something a trifle unseemly about the grownup who donned a witch costume each year, but we gladly drank the spicy brew she ladled from a washtub. Cavorting in the chill October air, crisp as the turning leaves under our feet, we knew each brightly shining doorway waited on our pleasure.

So the childhood Halloweens whirled by in a blur of sweets and mummery. Only on dream's outer fringes clung the shadow of a wicker carriage curved like a sea wave. I married, had children of my own, lived the yearly masquerade over again. And what a number I did! Handmade costumes, giant pumpkins from the country to carve into smiles, juicy apples slathered in caramel, and more parties than you could shake a broomstick at.

Then something began to happen to Halloween. At first it was just an isolated incident—a grisly newspaper item to shake off with a shudder. But the next year the stories multiplied, and suddenly the horror of razor blades concealed in apples brought to mind the dark side of fairy tales. We sent our children off to "trick or treat," but now the homemade goodies were suspect.

Who could tell? The cider-and-doughnut lady might be a female Scrooge warming up for Christmas; a candy apple might hide a lethal heart. When the kids brought their loot back home, we dumped the contents on the kitchen table and made them discard any candy that didn't come in a commercial wrapper. The year my youngest announced she was too old to go begging on Halloween, I shed no tears over childhood's end.

Now our children are grown and live in houses of their own; the quiet we sometimes prayed for turns in on us like a curse. I feel October in the air again. For weeks, plastic bags of candy decorated for Halloween have crowded the shelves of supermarkets and drugstores. I find myself resenting the exorbitant cost of the packaged candies I feel forced to buy. Still, if I baked chocolate-chip cookies and offered them for old time's sake, what child would be allowed to eat them?

Last Halloween, I turned off the porch light early and let the door bell ring . . . and ring. Sickened by the sound, I was reminded of how I felt when my children were small and the doctor advised letting them "cry it out." This October 31, I might just close up the house and go to the movies. A funny thing: I've been dreaming about the wicker carriage again lately, but when I awake, I can never remember if I was pushing it . . . or being pushed.

WHEN I MARRIED AT EIGHTEEN, I CAR-
ried my books and clothes from my father's house
directly into the lodgings I was to share with my
new husband. I had never held a job or been
away from home for more than a week. Few expectations were shattered by what was then a
conventional move. Like many young women in
my high school, a diamond engagement ring to
flash during senior year, the promise of babies
and a little home in the suburbs, were expecta-
tion enough for me.

I got that home, and four babies eventually,
and soon found myself trapped in a maze of
identical houses on an anonymous cul-de-sac,
houses inhabited by young women like myself.
We spent our days applying the contents of various bottles and jars to the furniture, floors, and
babies we had wanted so badly.

My husband came home each night, at first from college and then from a budding law practice, to find a wife with as little to say as the vegetables he was trying to grow in the inhospitable builder's sand of our backyard. I remember mornings when my youngest son rocked his crib from wall to wall, leaving mounds of cracked plaster on the floor, while I burrowed under the covers until noon, desperately trying to pass the hours away.

The articles and advice columns I read in newspapers and woman's magazines warned me about wives who failed to keep their husbands "interested." But who could be interested in someone who bored herself to tears? I made out long reading lists I was forever losing and clipped diet plans I read carefully as I gorged on the baked goods my father brought on each of his weekend visits.

But diapers give way to training pants, and I found time to become a neighborhood volunteer, collecting for this and that, eager for conversation, curious about the interchangeable kitchens into which I was invited by tired women who could have been me.

One afternoon while we watched our children play in the neighborhood schoolyard, another young mother and I began talking. For hours we laughed and chattered, ignoring the plucking hands and whining voices, commiserating, discovering correspondences, beginning a friendship.

A few days later, leaving our children with our husbands, my new friend and I braved dark highways to the county seat for a political meeting. There was a small matter of large potholes we wanted repaired. I left that meeting with a long list of names to telephone and the clearest sense of purpose I had experienced in a long time.

Well, we elected a highway commissioner who repaired our roads, and I had something to do with the victory. I still followed the advice columns, but now I read the editorial page first. Our oldest went off to kindergarten, and I cried, but not for long. I was too busy scheduling coffee hours in our subdivision for the state legislature candidate.

My husband and I found we had to take turns discussing our day. Sometimes we never got to his turn at all. Crazily, the more I did, the more I found time and energy for. The children grew before our eyes, and I did, too. For ten years I worked in politics; I call that decade "my first life."

When my husband landed a job in Washington, I dragged my feet. What would I do without a ringing telephone, meetings to attend, my network of friends and relatives? For six months I slumped back to my early marriage days, resentful of the change, and then I decided a new life was in order. It was time to go to college. When my youngest enrolled in kindergarten, I signed up for an English course at the local university.

I worried about everything. What if I had to write a paper? It had been fifteen years since I left high school. What would eighteen-year-olds make of a thirty-five-year-old freshman? A classroom wasn't a political meeting. Would I have the nerve to ask a question or venture an opinion? How many of my brain cells were already dead?

By the time I was forty, I had my B.A. with special honors and was barreling toward a master's degree. I wrote papers, studied for exams while my kids did their homework, and drank coffee in the student cafeteria with dozens of fellow students half my age.

When my colleagues began applying for teaching assistantships, I wondered why I couldn't try for one also. Too old, I told myself, anticipating probable rejection. I got the assistantship, could now finance my own education, found I was a fine teacher. I began to realize there was little I couldn't do if I really wanted to.

One spring day, I stood at the major cross-streets of my university and wept. I had just finished the comprehensive exams for a doctorate in American literature. Perhaps I wept from relief. The grueling months of study were over at last. I know I also cried because another one of my lives was over, and I couldn't bear for it to end.

Shortly afterward, I was offered the position of middle-school director in a small private school nearby. I had no teacher's certificate, had taken no education courses, and had no formal administrative experience. Our youngest child was in junior high by then. The floors in my house waited to be scrubbed; the furniture polish beckoned. But so did another life. I took the job, my first full-time position, and have been working at it and loving it for ten years.

At fifty-two, I feel younger than I did back in our little tract house when I tried to sleep the hours away. Each morning I arise with a sense of anticipation that the day confirms. I don't know how many more lives are left to me, but surely there will be others, and whatever they are, I will try to be open to them.

I have learned that physical change, though superficial, is inexorable. There is nothing we can do to stop it. What matters is that the intellect and spirit can change as well, and we do have the power to affect such change. So I look forward to my future lives, pray my health remains good, and promise myself the certain rewards of a life that is always becoming.

IF THIS IS THE "TELL IT LIKE IT IS" GEN-eration, count me out. Doesn't anyone opt for hypocrisy anymore? Whatever became of the delights of dissembling, the euphoria brought on by a well-chosen euphemism? Frankly, the naked truth, the bare facts, and letting it all hang out make me want to run for cover, and I come by this attitude naturally.

Had there been an Olympics division for the white lie, my father would have brought home the gold. He was my mentor, my coach. "Tell all the Truth but tell it Slant—," says the poet, Emily Dickinson. Daddy would have understood that. "Success in Circuit lies. . . ."

My father chain-smoked Luckies, and he suffered through the Sabbath and other Jewish holy days when the lighting of fire was prohibited. At least I *thought* he suffered, until one Yom Kippur during which the stifling women's balcony of our Orthodox synagogue began to feel like a Turkish bath. I *had* to get some fresh air.

Outside, halfway down the block, I spotted our Chevy, parked before sundown the night before, waiting for the holiday to be over so we could drive it home. A whisper of smoke trailed from an open window. I panicked. Our car was on fire! I didn't even know if it was all right to extinguish a fire on Yom Kippur; everything *else* was prohibited.

I ran to the smoking car and looked inside. There on the back seat, fully stretched out, was my diminutive father, puffing on a cigarette. "Shhh," he said, inhaling deeply. "What they don't know won't hurt them." "They" were my Orthodox grandparents. My father was more certain of God's forgiveness than of theirs.

A grand master at getting along, Daddy always managed to warn me before he brought his parents out to visit my husband and me in our first home. We lived in a little tract house in what were then the wilds of Oakland County just outside Detroit. I recall one particular day when he called from a gas station to tell me I had ten minutes to make the house "kosher" before he and Bobbe and Zayde arrived. I swept, dusted, straightened, and then, as the doorbell rang, I remembered those fat little pink slices. The bacon!

I grabbed the incriminating package from the fridge, considered stuffing it in my underpants, and instead, slam-dunked it down the clothes chute. Nowadays, I suppose we would have all sat around having a colloquy on whether or not it was everyone's right to do his own thing. Not then. My grandmother could have outpointed Golda Meir in the Knesset. You didn't *win* arguments with her; you *survived* them.

So I put on the teakettle. My father lit up a Lucky and leaned back expansively. Helping Bobbe to some strawberry jam to sweeten her tea, I glanced at him. His face was impassive. Then I noticed his left hand resting on the table. I'm sure only the two of us knew why my father's index and middle fingers were so carefully crossed.

YOU WILL RECOGNIZE THE KIND OF DAY IT
was: out of milk the night before, all-night supermarket at 6:30 A.M., full day's work, week's grocery shopping on my lunch hour, a yogurt wolfed
with a plastic spoon at 3:00 P.M., and there I was
in my driveway at last, trying to figure out how I
could get all those groceries into the house in less
than four trips. My mother-in-law, as usual, was
waiting for me at the front door. "Faye," she said
wistfully as one of the overloaded bags slipped
out of my arms, "how come you don't bake apple
pies no more?"

I tell this story not to boast that I am a latter-
day Charlie Chaplin straight out of *Modern
Times* but to make a confession instead. That
evening, when I returned from a parents' meeting, I bought some apples and baked those pies.
After living with my mother-in-law for over thirty

years, I was still trying to prove that I was a better housewife than she was.

My mother-in-law became a widow within weeks after her son and I joined hands under the wedding canopy. We stayed with her for several months and then, wisely, decided to buy our own house and find an apartment in which my mother-in-law could begin life anew. Unfortunately, she was already hooked on pain pills prescribed for a chronic physical ailment and, in addition, was taking advantage of what was then the usual widow's sop: a refillable prescription for sleeping pills.

The telephone, like a time bomb, waited next to our bed. "I heard a crash next door. You better come. I think your mother's fallen again." We could have made that frantic drive to her apartment in our sleep. Some nights, I think, we virtually did.

Gradually my mother-in-law began spending her days at our house. After a while we stopped playing games and she moved in with us. It seemed a reasonable trade-off: the knife-in-the-gut phone calls in exchange for a good night's sleep. That's how simple it was. She has been with us ever since and, as Robert Frost says, "That has made all the difference."

No strangers to extended families, my husband

and I both grew up in homes with resident grand-parents. My mother's father was a miser who sewed his savings into his underwear. On Saturday nights my poor brother was given the hazardous chore of sneaking into the bathroom to confiscate the soiled union suit during Grandfather's enforced weekly bath. The anguished cries of "Thief!" that ensued and the frantic scrabbling in the clothes hamper made bedlam of our weekends.

My husband's grandmother was a four-and-one-half-foot harridan who slept in the living room. Her tiny body seemed to occupy no space at all, and yet she was everywhere—into cooking pots, closets, and would-be private conversations.

You can bet that neither my husband nor I had any Norman Rockwell illusions about mixing the generations when we invited his mother to live with us. Still, I remember the early years with my mother-in-law as peaceful ones. The four children who followed, a house to clean, my husband's busy life as a neighborhood lawyer, and my own deep involvement in volunteer political work—all welcomed an extra pair of willing hands and a built-in baby-sitter. Of course, I worried about my mother-in-law's dependency on us, but there were other concerns. Sometimes I had trouble deciding exactly where I stood in that blurry family photo: mother, daughter, wife. Roles were not merely reversing in our house; they were doing backflips.

When we moved to Washington, we gave thought to leaving my mother-in-law behind in Detroit. She was scarcely sixty years old then, but her health, though improved, was still fragile, and in our youthful omniscience we were certain she would be better off living with us. So we took her to Washington and made permament a condition we had always pretended was temporary.

By this time our youngest child was ready for kindergarten. Suddenly my mother-in-law and I found ourselves, women of different generations, stuck all day in the same echoing, empty house. My mother-in-law, with nothing to do, stepped on my heels; she sulked on the front porch like an abandoned child when I went out to escape her. Instead of partners, we became antagonists, struggling for control of a few feet of disputed territory: the kitchen. Lingering over morning coffee became an endurance contest for me. How many times could I bear to be interrupted by a lonely old woman before I stomped upstairs to barricade myself behind a slammed bedroom door?

Our children grew older; we met around the dinner table at night and then, polarized, scattered to the chill of our respective rooms. Privacy: we hungered for it, would have worn the word like a button on our lapels, marched with it on a placard, had we been able. My mother-in-law's increasing deafness isolated her further. We turned our backs to her when we talked, spoke in whispers, closed another door against her.

I enrolled at a university, got a B.A. and an M.A., passed my comprehensives for a Ph.D. We joked that Grandma's name ought to be on the diploma since her presence had forced me out of the house to get those degrees. But we pushed her out of the nest, too, to senior citizens' groups, to Jewish women's organizations. Reluctantly at first and then with increasing anticipation she went, forgetting her aches and pains in the excitement of her new life. We all grew, made compromises, adjusted.

It still isn't easy. I haven't stopped railing at the bit of kosher soap and frayed steel-wool pad my mother-in-law leaves on the sink when she cleans the pots she insists no one can shine as she does. At least now I admit that I don't like to scrub pots, and we no longer have jurisdictional disputes about it. I realize that old people are stubborn; so am I. I still have to explain to my mother-in-law what I'm doing and where I'm going, but I do it not as a rebellious daughter hoarding my mite of privacy but as an adult responsible for the well-being of another. My own daughters, who live nearby, call on their grandmother every few days; my out-of-town sons write to her and phone her every week. So much of their lives is bound up in hers.

The last time my mother-in-law fell and shattered yet another brittle bone, my husband and I both wept. "We're stuck with her," we agreed, and there's been no more frivolous talk of an apartment with a companion or senior citizens' homes. Instead of counting her years as we often used to do, we sit with her around our diminished dinner table and are grateful for each healthy day she spends involved in her activities.

My mother-in-law's presence has added a dimension to my life without which I would have been quite another person. Her energy, the lust to live she discovered so late, her love for her son and our children and their love for her; her love for me and, finally, yes, my love for her, all sustain me now as I reach the age she was when she came into my home. At eighty, she is no longer a resented permanent resident but a guest in our house, one whose time of departure is uncertain but inevitable.

KENNEDY TO FRANKFURT, FRANKFURT TO Geneva, Geneva to Nice: everything on schedule, each transfer smooth as tissue paper. Time after time I checked the contents of my purse, ticked them off like staples on a grocery list: tickets, baggage claim checks, passport, travelers' checks, address book. Sophisticated world traveler, fifty years old, and off to France for three months, away from husband, children, home . . . on my own.

At Nice airport a bit of my glittering bravado flaked away. No husband to run interference for me on this trip. Shlepping three heavy bags up and down flights of stairs whose architectural purpose eluded me washed further starch out of my resolve. I felt like timid Frieda from Jacques Brel: "There she goes with her valises, held so tightly in her hand." Blinding neon bouncing off stainless steel, the babel of unfamiliar languages, and, finally, no answer at the foundation in Vence where I was to spend the next months writing reduced me to a blob of crème caramel.

I gathered together the butt ends of my jet-lagged confidence and, my schoolgirl French assaulting my own ears, made a reservation at a hotel in Nice. Once safely at the hotel, bathed, in bed eating a hard roll squirreled away from lunch, a book and cigarettes close by, I experienced a contentment so profound that it rivaled any in my memory. In the anonymity of that room, my whereabouts unknown to anyone in the world save the concierge, who cared only that I pay in advance, I was for the first time in my life truly alone.

In anticipation of a sabbatical year away from the small high school where I teach, I began early to tongue the delicious possibilities available to me. My hedonistic bent warred with my pragmatic slant. "Have a good time," one side said, "but be productive," chimed in the other. When a friend suggested a writers' colony in the south of France, I casually sent off an application the way one floats a letter in a bottle, with little hope of response. I did not seem to fit the colony's profile of previous residents (the brochure called for young artists), and, besides, the notion of three months far away from my home and family was too remote for me to contemplate seriously.

Still, the possibility toyed with me, wouldn't let me go. There was no sleep-over camp in my background, no going away to college. Out of high school into marriage, I found the fragile filaments of husband, then children, combining to weave a web seductive and strong enough to have kept me bound for more than thirty years.

I felt ashamed of my longing to get free for a little while, disloyal and unappreciative of what I was fortunate enough to possess. And I had witnessed at close remove the unbidden loneliness of widowhood, the punishing solitude of divorce. My desire to get off by myself seemed to mock the agony of women I knew who, halved, were struggling for wholeness again.

My husband was with me when the answer came from France. We were sitting over morning coffee one Saturday, sharing items from the newspaper, parceling out chores for the shiny day that lay ahead. I turned over the blue envelope in my hands, preparing myself (with a sense of relief) for the disappointment. "Here's the rejection slip from the foundation," I told my husband, waving the letter at him. It wasn't a rejection at all, of course, and suddenly I was drenched by a wash of homesickness for the very kitchen in which I sat.

"Well, anyway," I said, "I don't see how I could possibly just take off and *leave* everybody."

As women we are so often defined by who leans on us. Being needed names us: wife, mother, teacher, nurse. But, after a while, those leaners become our props as well. As with unfinished houses, there is a danger that we might collapse if our props are removed too soon. I told myself I couldn't go to France because of my responsibility to those who leaned on me. When I finally did go, it was because I wanted to test my own foundations, wanted to discover whether, unpropped, I could stand alone. "Have a good time," my oldest daughter told me as we kissed goodbye, "and don't mother anybody!"

There were ten of us, artists and writers, scattered in small cabins and houses on a generous sun-dappled estate in Vence, fifteen minutes from Nice in the south of France. I was the oldest resident, the only married person, and one of two women, the other being young enough to be my daughter. Our social pool was tiny. I wondered if the others would like me and then remembered I had come to France to explore the limits of seclusion.

As I dropped my luggage in the living room of the prefab cottage that was to be my home for the next three months, the words of an old folk song moiled in my ears: "What was your name in the States?" In a strange, small way I was replicating what my immigrant parents had done sixty years before me; like them I was starting a fresh life in a foreign country. I was alone, without family or friends. In France I was no one's anything. My fellow residents would have only my self to measure me by. I sloughed off yesterday like old skin.

At first my days had no spine to give them shape, no job to awaken for, no children to check in with on the phone, no husband to share my supper in the evening. Slowly I constructed an armature of tasks, fleshed it out with periods of rest and walks to town. Guilt got me up in the morning, but a pleasant exhaustion put me to bed at night. Each familiar act, transplanted, took on a luster reflected off my solitude and fresh surroundings. Broken down to their elements and closely considered, drinking a cup of fragrant coffee became a communion, a bouquet of pink carnations for my room, an offering. My cabin was crowded with my aloneness.

I shopped for food and cooked and wrote and slept, shared wine and conversation with my fellow residents. Day to night and back again, the hours shot through, silver shuttles, weaving a pattern of my own design. I threw my watch away, awakened when the sun reached my eye- lids, ate when I felt empty, climbed into bed sometimes at seven to wrap myself against the bone chill of the star-filled nights.

Bits of home arrived in the mail: letters, tapes, photographs, newspaper clippings of hostages re- leased, attempted assassinations, everything in slow motion; we were sometimes weeks apart. I wrote back. I thought of my husband and chil- dren but, to my immense surprise, found the pain of missing them dulled by distance. Too far away from them to affect their lives directly, I began to believe they could survive without me and I without them. Crazily, none of us were dimin- ished in the process.

I came home from France two weeks early so my family and I could be together for Passover, my favorite of the Jewish holidays. Thoreau spent two years and two months in the woods. I man- aged just ten weeks. In a way I resented losing those few extra days, but I was alone long enough to realize that the woods are a state of mind. Even today I am sustained by the memory of liv- ing for a time "deliberately." Like Thoreau, "at present I am a sojourner in civilized life again," but my confrontation with what he calls the "essential facts" has shown me that, even shorn of props, the house I inhabit is sound, inside and out.

THE MATRIARCHS GROW OLD, MY MODELS, women who were women when I was a child. Who will be left to call me "Faygele" when they are no longer here? With no one but me to recall my childhood, who will validate the memories? They will carry pieces of me when they go. How much of their strength will they bequeath to me? The years pass, and the distance between us collapses in fan folds; one day I will be standing where they are now. . . .

Home, after work, I turn on the answering machine, pen in hand, to note the names and numbers. A buzz, and then Aunt Lena's voice floats out of the recorder, no ear to cup the sound before it fills the room. "I'm sorry to be the one to tell you this," she begins, and I feel defenseless, somehow, against the disembodied message.

"Aunt Rachel passed away last night," she says. Where are the muffled drumbeats, the clamor of bells? Only this scratchy old-time radio voice, trapped in vinyl tape.

I call my husband to impart the news, discuss with him the best way to inform his aged mother that her sister-in-law is dead. His mother has had a hard winter, and we are fearful of jarring her fragile equilibrium. We decide to tell her at dinner, the first time we will be together again that day.

Seated at the table, we avoid her eyes, drop our glances away from the shaking hands, attenuate the time until the announcement. It hurts to imagine how she must feel, on the firing line of old age, wondering if she will be the next to fall. "Let's get it over with," my husband mutters. His mother doesn't hear him; she is quite deaf.

I will be the one to say it, I tell myself. Perhaps I can phrase the words more gently than he can. But I quail at the deafness, the problem of delivering bad news at the top of my lungs. The possibility of nuance is gone; I cannot soften the harsh words by a lowering of the voice or the gloss of inflection.

"Ma," I say at last, raising my voice. "Rachel passed away; Aunt Lena called." The piece of bread is halfway to her mouth, and she continues to carry it in one unbroken sweep.

"Tough woman," my husband says of his aunt.

"Rachel was a cossack!" his mother affirms.

I look her full in the face now. She is dry-eyed, a tough woman, too.

I wonder how tough *I* am, now that the years stretch behind me in a swath sufficient to reveal texture and design. Are there surprises left? My responses seem to me these days as predictable as the tobacco-covered pennies that turn up at the bottom of my purse. The women of whom I speak: their lives were tempered by pogroms, the blast from the gas ovens. They endured loss of land and language, answered to "Greenhorn" before they knew what the word meant. By contrast with them, my life has reached the soft-ball stage in the likes of a jelly kettle. I pray I never endure their crucible, but I covet the nature of their strength.

The world tastes flat—meat without salt, more often than not. I know how fortunate I am to have been born in my own special time and place. Still, that doesn't cheer me when I get the blues any more than the example of starving babies in China ever made leftover food more palatable when I was a child. I ponder the years to come and see mixed messages wherever I go. . . .

Three elderly ladies share a bench at the neighborhood supermarket, crocheted shopping bags and metal carts tucked at their sides. Dressed for the season, they sport dark, flowered polyester dresses, good wool coats, and tidy hats. The few minutes of gossip they exchange add importance to an errand already blown out of proportion by the meagerness of their days.

A similarly clad shopper passes the seated group and calls to one of the bench warmers. "Hi, neighbor," she says. A blank look for response, and then, "Why, I didn't recognize you!" Halfway to the exit, the first calls back crisply, "You never do." "Well," says the seated neighbor in self-defense, "You've changed so." Shoulders slumping, the departing woman mumbles to no one in particular, "Don't I know it!"

At fifty-two, I feel changes also. Not since my teens, the years when we are all eager for the clock to speed up, have birthdays provoked such introspection. I was conscious of the passage of time back then in a way the intervening years have never mirrored. Too busy, perhaps, bearing babies, raising them, finally growing up myself, to watch the clock.

For a long time, I approached birthdays calmly, counting out the comfortable number of years I could reasonably expect according to the biblical formula (as good a measure as any), and always the three score years and ten allowed me more than half of what I had already eaten up. After I reached the "halfway" mark, I changed the rules and began to measure by actuarial tables; still there was comfort in the numbers. Now, add and subtract as I may, the balance is against me. I find more years gone than I can hope to have in store.

For the first time, I wish I had some of those years to live over again. That beautiful decade between forty and fifty: I wouldn't waste it sleeping so much, dreaming, staring at walls, doing crossword puzzles, listening to the stories of people I don't really care very much about. Things are different now that the moon is no longer my timekeeper. The depressions can't be so easily explained away by a knowing glance at the calendar. I wonder if I have time left to write a novel; will I ever shape the hoarded bits of brightly colored fabric into the quilt I always thought I'd make one day?

The hair I swore I'd never cut, "until I die," I playfully said, hangs heavy, makes me question long-range promises. My daughter told me tactfully not long ago, "They have great hair coloring now; you should really think about it." I do. My students beg me to let my hair hang loose instead of in a knot, and I brush them away like insistent flies. I don't want to look like the women I see in the country with Dolly Parton pompadours and sagging faces underneath. Nevertheless, I understand about outer changes. What Robert Frost calls "inner weather" concerns me more.

The days whirl by in a rhythm of their own, free-wheeling, out of my control. I grab at the nights with my fingertips and cannot hold on. Be productive, I tell myself, not certain any longer just what my quota is. I write, I teach, I mother and wife, I eat and drink and read. But my shadow shortens and threatens to catch up with me. I look to the matriarchs for their secrets and see they are falling. They speak to me with words that echo Eliot's *Wasteland*. HURRY UP, they say. HURRY UP PLEASE IT'S TIME.

My mother sits in a straight-backed chair, holding me wedged in the V of her knees while she secures a button hanging like a loose tooth from my skirt placket. "Bite the string," she urges, and I grip the bit of thread she has given me to chew so the devil will not "sew up my sense."

Along with the featherbeds and brass Sabbath candles she brought from the old country, my mother carried her old wives' tales. My daily life was sprinkled with superstition as thickly as poppy seeds on a kaiser roll. If I stepped over one of my brothers as he lay on the carpet rolling a toy truck, my mother warned me to step right back over so as not to stunt his growth. A baby, hers or anyone else's, she invariably pronounced "ugly." Why alert the evil eye to the whereabouts of a beautiful child? She tossed a little ball of dough into the oven with the *challah* to propitiate the evil spirits and ensure a perfect loaf. Onions were sliced from top to bottom: bad luck to cut off their heads. Ladybugs who found their way into the house were protected: good luck to have them around. My childhood was a bundle tied up in the kerchief of her superstitions. It is not nostalgia but the insistence of memory that makes me speak of them now.

The stink of fear danced around her head always, like a swarm of gnats. Danger was everywhere. If it wasn't the Angel of Death or the evil eye, it was infantile paralysis lurking in the cool Michigan lakes, VD on public toilet seats, broken limbs from skates and bikes; every stranger was a potential child molester. The wonder was she didn't insist on sitting in my classrooms. She certainly walked me to school until I was old enough to make her trail half a block behind me so my classmates wouldn't know what she was up to. Early on, she chalked a circle of dread around us all and grew hysterical if any of us stepped over the line.

My mother's demons kept her in her place. Anxiety enough in the familiar without advertising for trouble. Cooking and cleaning were her touchstones. For a woman, a shining house and shining children were enough. Still she told me

once, shyly, she hoped I would be a newspaper-
woman when I grew up, like Lorelei Kilburne, a
fictional character who wrote for the *Illustrated
Press* on a popular radio show. She surprised me
that day. It hadn't occurred to me that she might
see in my life an opportunity to break out of the
constricting circle.

I married, vaguely yearning for something different from what my mother had, but unable to
define it, much less articulate it. Hard now to accept how ignorant I was about my options, how
imprisoned I was in a world little removed from
my mother's jungle of superstition and the old
wives' tales many of my contemporaries dis-
paraged but secretly half believed. Like other
first-generation daughters, I saw marriage as an
escape from the smothering atmosphere of the
ghetto; where I was going wasn't as important as
getting out. But I soon discovered distance was
no synonym for difference.

My cousins, and most other young married
women I knew during the early fifties, swore by a
fatherly obstetrician whose popularity was based
on his reputation for "painless" deliveries. Preg-
nant with my first child, I, too, sought him out as
a matter of course. I was anxious to please him
and counted myself fortunate if he patted my
fanny at the end of an office visit and said, "Good

girl," when I hadn't gained too much weight. That and a reassuring "Everything's fine!" seemed communication enough between us. Childbirth was something women whispered about in the kitchen. I never got the impression anyone had much control over it, and I certainly wasn't going to bother my busy doctor with a shopping list of complaints and questions.

I remember the early stages of labor; we played cribbage, my husband and I, but when things began to get serious, he was hustled out. I think I was glad to see him go. The woman behind the screen in the bed next to mine screamed and screamed. "Mama, you were right," she kept hollering. "Mama, you were right!" I was embarrassed for her, told myself no matter what happened, I would never carry on like that. Still, she unnerved me, and the vestiges of my confidence began to crumble like stale bread.

Who knows, finally, what I did? "Had enough?" the fatherly obstetrician asked when the contractions began to flow together in one monumental wave. "Oh, yes," I said, and after the anesthetic, my recollection is pieced together out of the fabric of nightmare. I remember an iron bed with sides pulled up like a crib, a sense of my body out of control. From somewhere far away, I heard conversation, laughter . . . no urgency. A telephone rang in another place. Under me, sheets swam in warm water. Had I wet the bed? My God. The helpless feeling of being a naughty child. I wanted to please everyone, and now this.

Through it all, the pulling. Would they ever stop pulling me? I hear the voice of my doctor. Did I dream it? "She has been a fine patient, a good girl." Oh, yes, tell me that, and then I am climbing the crib, one leg over the side. "And where do you think you're going?" the woman in white asks, brusquely. I am crying now, like the screaming woman, making a spectacle of myself. I have been a failure. . . .

My eyes open to a world of white walls and stainless steel fixtures. Ahead of me, a round clock tells the hour, but without my glasses the numbers are fuzzy black patches. My watch and wedding rings are gone, too, and suddenly I place my hands on my middle. The baby that had leaped like a fish under my heart . . . gone, my belly like an empty dish. Now I realize where I am. A white uniform fingers my wrist. "I thought you'd never wake up," she says.

Well, like a lot of other women, I have been waking up ever since. My four children are grown now. I will pass down to them the red apple dishes and the dining room set my mother bought on the installment plan. But I won't pass along the ignorance and fear that slammed doors every way she turned. Make no mistake, I know it was love for me that made her try to protect me from the real dangers of this world as well as the chimeras whose existence she could only imagine.

I have protected my children, too, but I am content that the weapons I used were more formidable than avoidance and superstition. I have tried to teach them what I have learned: that risk is no excuse for inaction nor custom a definition of boundaries.

Now THAT I HAVE REACHED FIFTY, I FIND myself, more and more, stepping outside myself to see what is becoming of me. As my body thickens and my face seems to thumb its nose at the kindness of cosmetics, I select from the trick-or-treat bag of my memory a feature here, a character trait there. I notice that I place my thumb on my chin, my fingers on my temple when I listen, just the way my father did, twist my Bobbe Stollman's skinny brown hair into a knot at the back of my head. Some matches are obvious, but it has taken me years to realize that one of the women I have been becoming all along is an incarnation of the Pushke Lady.

Winter Sunday mornings in Detroit, my father and I would walk to the Warsaw Bakery on Twelfth Street to buy bagels. After cold that bit like an ax blade, runny noses, ice squeaking beneath our galoshes, we would stand inside the cinnamon-scented steam box until the fog on our glasses cleared enough for us to make the familiar choices from freshly laden bins and boxes piled high with crusty rolls and sugary cakes. No matter how early we came, the Pushke Lady was there before us, sitting in a chair safely out of the draft, shaking her canister under our noses. Jewish National Fund, Pioneer Women, Hadassah, milk for Jewish orphans, trees for Palestine— thanks to the Pushke Lady, no Jew would have to slather cream cheese on his bagel with a guilty conscience.

During the Depression, when we moved to a little town not far from Detroit, spring brought the tramps, pale and spindly, looking like plants do when they have had to reach too far to find the sun. Coming home from school, I would often spot a man at the back door looking for odd jobs, slouch hat or cotton cap held in both hands over his chest, hungry, and my mother would feed him: cold potatoes, bread, coffee; we had little enough ourselves. Drying her hands on a dish towel just inside the screened door, she would listen to the story as though she had not heard one like it many times before. Miraculously, she always had a dollar or two put away from what

my father gave her. Her *knippl,* she called it, and
more than once I saw her fish out a dime or a
quarter from the old Droste's cocoa box where
she kept it to send on his way a tramp whose
story had particularly touched her heart. Afterward she would tell me, as though making excuses, "It's a *mitzvah* to feed the poor."

Our house was a regular stop for pious men in
need of a kosher meal who might find themselves
without time enough to reach Detroit or Chicago
before sundown of a Friday night. "You're doing
a *mitzvah,*" my mother would say when I grumbled about giving up my bed to a stranger. What
has become of them, those grizzled men in long
black coats, poring over yellowed prayer books by
the light of our living room window on Shabbes
mornings so long ago? My mother would believe
they were in heaven now, saying prayers for all of
us.

I reached adolescence just before the creation
of the Jewish state, and although my family still
felt, then, that Jews should wait for the messiah
to carry them back to Israel, they did not put on
sackcloth when I joined the Labor Zionist movement. Certainly I was doing what I had been
brought up to do when I stood on a street corner
holding a canister, vying with the newsboys for

their customers' change. This time a new cause benefited, but the Pushke Lady's spirit hovered above me, crowing over every coin.

As a young married, locked into a small suburban community by babies and a lack of transportation, I met my fellow prisoners by collecting door to door for the Torch Drive, the name given to the United Way campaign in Michigan. In kitchen after kitchen, twin to my own, I drank coffee, shared recipes and surprising intimacies with barely postadolescent women like myself. Almost always, I came away with a few dollars in my envelope to justify my visit and the sense that I had performed a *mitzvah* to justify my life.

The children grew, and I collected: Dollars for Democrats, March of Dimes on Roosevelt's birthday, UNICEF on Halloween. Later, the Pushke Lady syndrome became more complicated. When my oldest daughter was sixteen, I took her with me to the Alabama state capital to meet the Freedom Marchers who had walked from Selma to Montgomery. We both still remember the voice of Martin Luther King floating over our heads in the electric air and the long, sober train ride back with blinds drawn and lights out for fear of snipers. I didn't tell my daughter the trip was a *mitzvah* or even that it was part of her *pushke* training, but she knows it now.

118

Living in Washington during the sixties, we made our home a way station for peace marchers. The spaghetti pot bubbled, and the sleeping bags came out at the drop of a bullhorn. We offered Band-Aids for blistered feet, legal aid for those arrested, and telephoned more than one hysterical parent to report a son or daughter in good hands. I have met people, perfect strangers, who accurately describe the inside of our house and tell me they were drop-ins for this march or that. *They* may not realize they stand at the head of a symbolic queue that began for me with an old man who carried a prayer book in his satchel— but I do.

Fund-raising is computerized now; we're not quick to let strangers into our homes, and no one seems to be marching very much, but the Pushke Lady in me still believes the *knippl* makes a difference. The world grows larger and more complex, yet hunger and pain have not lost their simplicity or directness. Besides, the way things are, I need to store up all the *mitzvahs* I can get.

I REALIZE AS I GROW OLDER THAT I REACH back more and more to the clear waters of my childhood. There, magnified rather than diminished by memory, my first teachers retain their freshness and power. Though many of them never set foot in a formal classroom, their lessons continue to sustain me; their methods undergird my philosophy of teaching. I am the sum of their feeling and doing.

I think of my earliest teachers, my grandfather, Dovid Shlomo, who could pare an apple in one long scarlet spiral or sharpen a pencil stub to a razor point with the same mother-of-pearl-handled penknife. Enchanted, I would watch him until the spell was broken by the feel of saliva dripping from my open mouth. My Bobbe Broche, a magician, caused snowflakes to grow from a crochet hook and a ball of string. What

magician shares secrets? She did. Fridays before
the Sabbath, she taught me, as she'd taught my
mother, to bake bread, to braid the *challah*, coat
it with egg yolk for a mahogany crust, and most
exciting of all, to ward off the evil eye with a tiny
ball of dough thrown to the back of the oven.
(That the bit of dough tested the oven tempera-
ture in a time of no thermostats was a practical
lesson I received as a bonus.)

These long-ago teachers found the patience to
help me with skills that move a child over from
infancy to childhood. They taught me to tie my
shoes, button my clothes, thread a needle, part
my hair. Always there was time, ". . . To take my
waking slow. . . ." Always my desire to know was
mirrored in their willingness to guide me.

I was always just a little afraid of my Zayde
Laybe. From the women's balcony of the Blaine
Shul, I could spot him standing next to the bench
where his grown sons sat on the Sabbath and
other holy days. When I could escape the women
with their wadded tear-soaked handkerchiefs, I
would have to duck under his frown to squeeze
past garbardine knees until I reached the sanc-
tuary of my father's lap. Countless times I
watched my grandfather take the black-bound
prayer book in his hands, raise it to his lips, and
then reverently open it. Sometimes it seems to

me I have always felt the rush of love I experience whenever I open a book, but my heart knows it was a pious grandfather who taught me that love.

Jenny and Essie Wood kept a cut-glass bowl of dried rose petals on a polished table in their parlor. When we became neighbors, I was five, not yet old enough to be ashamed of the garlic-and-onion smell that lurked in our lace curtains or insinuated itself into the stuffing of our cut-velour davenport, but old enough to be transported whenever I was invited next door.

The two women, both so old I could never remember which was the daughter of the other, welcomed me each afternoon at teatime as though I were an honored guest. They served me in see-through china cups instead of the heavy glasses from which we drank tea at home. They taught me to keep a napkin on my lap and to crook my little finger into a question mark as I held the cup. Together we had long, serious conversations. Like my grandparents, they listened to me and taught me to listen in return.

I learned the word "antique" at the Woods'. Years later, Henry James's *The Spoils of Poynton* evoked for me the possessions of those two ladies: the ironstone tureen with its delicate ladle curved like a sea wave, the tall clock whose hand-carved cherry works groaned as they moved to mark the hours, Great-Grandpa's crewel-embroidered wing chair, Great-Grandma's needle-pointed foot-stool. A taste for brass candlesticks and feather-beds was my inheritance; Jenny and Essie Wood wrapped my expectations in a Victorian crazy quilt that blazed like a stained-glass window.

When my family "lost everything" during the Depression, we moved in with Aunt Itke and Uncle Zaydl. Every morning before she began the cooking and cleaning for her husband, six children, and whoever else was living in her house at the time, Aunt Itke would put on a clean dress, "and not a house dress either," she would tell my mother. Then she, and later her daughters as they grew, would stand in front of a large mirror pinned to the wall with glass rosettes. She combed her shining auburn hair in the reflection of that mirror, fluffed the fringe cut over her forehead, and turned the side curls toward her cheeks. From little pots she colored her cheeks and lips and blackened her lashes with a tiny brush. They say she sleeps on her back to this day so her neck will not wrinkle, and more than forty years later (forgive me, Aunt Itke), she is beautiful still.

The dirt, seeping in from the junkyard that

was her husband's living and her home's back garden, never seemed to daunt her. Plants grew with confidence under her fingers; she talked to them long before it was fashionable. One day on her sun porch, surrounded by green plants and white wicker, she turned to me and said solemnly, "Faygele, never forget this: ferns love to drink tea." I haven't forgotten it or the feel of that house either.

Such a wonderful house it was in which to grow up. Where did she find the money for birthday cakes or the time to bake them? There were so many of us, it seemed candles blazed every week. Her talented fingers sewed bright covers for the secondhand furniture (and a doll's dress along the way for me); she crocheted doilies, stiffening them in sugar water until they formed lacy baskets for the center of a table. Always there was music in that house and laughter sometimes more than bread.

I have been fortunate in my teachers; I only name a handful here. More than anything their patience has inspired me to give my own children and my students time to breathe, time to take their waking slow. And yet, if I have learned anything, it is that we all change constantly from student to teacher and back again. My memory seems this moment like the Hall of Mirrors at Versailles, reflecting back in myriad number my face and the faces of my teachers. Backward and forward into infinity we go until my eye cannot distinguish my face from theirs.

FOR THREE DAYS AND NIGHTS IT RAINS, A cold, steady, inconsolable downpour. Water streams from slick tree branches where, a month earlier, drops might have pearled a moment before growing too heavy to hold on. On the streets, pockets of dead leaves pounded to blackened pulp are more treacherous underfoot than the snow their falling foretells.

That day my teacher had invited me to stay after school to help her clap erasers and wash the chalky blackboards with warm water and a sponge. Now the playground is empty; the puddled sidewalks, too, stretch before me, deserted, and up ahead are swallowed in the misty dusk. My mother will be looking for me, I know, and already my stomach clutches as, here and there, lamps are lit in the front rooms of houses I pass.

Ski suits are the fashion this Michigan fall of

1940. We girls call the bottoms "ski pants" and not "leggin's" and refuse to wear them anyway no matter how far the thermometer swallows its little red tongue. I have zipped my schoolbooks inside my ski jacket, and, bare-legged, hunch my shoulders against the ominous drumbeat of rain.

I'm hungry. The crust of peanut butter and jelly sandwich tossed in a wastebasket at lunchtime, ages ago, is worth a king's ransom this moment. I tell myself I could have survived for days on that tail end of bread if I had to.

And what if I have to? What if I get lost, take a wrong turn among these suddenly unfamiliar houses that seem to dissolve like sugar cubes as the rain intensifies, and darkness grips my shoulders with heavy hands? What if people have never heard of my street, or worse yet, refuse to answer their door at all?

At a lonely intersection where I am certain I have never been before, I stand next to the street sign and squint, trying to read the names, but in the failing light I can't make out the letters. My lace-up shoes squinch water; above my sopping, fallen-down knee socks, my thighs jump with cold, and worst of all, I have to pee. If only someone would walk by, I'd run the horrible risk of talking to strangers and ask where I am. No one comes.

By some miracle (and prayers, for I suddenly, deeply believe in God again—yes, a white-bearded, larger-than-life-sized God who sometimes smiles, but not often), I find myself on my own block, and then, the cold my mother is forever warning me about already scratching at the back of my throat, I am on my own front walk. In the doorway, a hand on her heart, is my mother. "You will kill me yet," she says. "You will be my finish, my end. Look at you! Where have you been?"

Piece by piece, I leave a trail of books, sodden shoes, soggy socks, my limp ski jacket, all the way to the bathroom. Now my skin begins to throb in the snug room. My mother has followed me. She rubs my hair dry in a rough towel. Her hands are angry. "I told you over and over: hat, scarf, mittens, boots, *leggin's!*" she shouts. And I find that the storm is inside, too. The mirror, where I sometimes see a dark-haired girl with a crooked part, is steamed over and faceless. The kitchen window, where I drew a heart with my finger only this morning, is blank now in the night and rain.

．　　　．　　　．

I spent a good part of my childhood getting ready to go blind. At night, I shuffled to the bathroom in the dark, my eyes screwed tightly shut, my arms outstretched in front of me, trying to memorize the floor plan of our house the way I memorized my lessons at school.

School was the real problem; there they were forever checking you out. Sometimes the county health nurse parted your hair with rubber-gloved fingers and searched for nits, whatever they were. The kids said if she found them, you might have to get your head shaved. They checked your teeth, too, and your feet to see if they were flat, and your ears.

All that was all right. Only the fear of the eye test kept me awake at night, for I knew I would fail, and sooner or later my parents would find out. They must have suspected something because my mother kept telling me I would ruin my eyes if I insisted on reading all the time. My father said, "You don't want to have to get glasses, do you? Who will want to marry a girl who wears glasses?" It didn't occur to me that he might be joking. Certainly I believed that *he* wouldn't have married me with glasses, and at the time, nothing much else mattered.

One day, poking in the room my grandfather shared with my brother, I came upon the lens from an old pair of glasses. I had no business messing in his dresser drawers and I knew it, but I filched the bit of glass and carried it to my bedroom, where I held it to my eye. It was a round lens, small as they were in those days, little bigger than a quarter. When I squinted my other eye, a miracle occurred: the fuzzy world leaped suddenly into focus. I looked out the window and for the first time saw the true shapes of leaves as they hung on the trees. I held the glass to my eye and looked in the mirror that hung on the door of the hall closet. There was a girl in the glass with her hand to her eye. I could see her entire body in sharp relief instead of the blurred figure who had always been reflected there before.

Heart pounding, I wrapped the glass circle in a bit of tissue and carried it in my fist downtown. I held it squinting to my eye again and read street signs, Mason Street, Elm, Franklin. I could make out advertising signs on fences and the sides of buildings: "Chew Mail Pouch Tobacco." "Fletcher's Castoria: Children Cry for It." I pressed my nose against Stillman's window and read the price tags pinned to the dummies. For the first time I could tell the hour from the clock on the wall of the comfort station instead of counting the church bells as they clanged, one set slightly after the other, in different parts of town.

Of course, the world through that glass circle looked different to me in other ways. There was a hard-edged reality to people and objects no longer softened by the halo of near-sightedness. I noticed the faint mustache above my aunt's beautiful lips, the freckles on each peach as it turned from green to rose in our backyard orchard. All my life I had perceived my surroundings through a filmy veil. Now I realized that nothing, no matter how perfect I had thought it to be, was unflawed.

My grandfather's little glass saw me through the next year or so. Each semester at school I failed the eye test, and every time I was handed a pink slip, I carefully folded it into a tiny square and flushed it down the toilet in the girls' lavatory. I squinted through the lens sometimes in class so I did not have to walk up to the front of the room where the blackboard was, and with my magnifying glass in front of my eye, I could see the movie from the middle of the theater instead of the first row, where my cousin Shirley never wanted to sit. I knew that looking through the stolen circle was bad for me. I would surely go blind now, sooner than ever.

The summer I was twelve, I began to baby-sit for a young couple who lived across the street from us. The husband was an eye doctor whose office was the converted front room of their house. For weeks he badgered my parents. "Let me examine her eyes," he said. He must have no-

ticed immediately how near-sighted I was. I felt
more terrified than ever that someone would finally tell my parents just how far from perfect I
really was. If my father didn't want a daughter
with glasses, what would he do with a blind girl?

One way or another, the doctor got me into his
office. With a tiny light that rested on his forehead like a miner's lamp, he peered into my eyes,
his cheek firmly pressed against mine. I felt faint
from his nearness, the male scent of leather on
which I sat, the cold instrument hard against my
face.

From a slotted tray, he slipped lens after lens
into a large machine that he swiveled like a sub-
marine periscope in front of my eyes. At last, the
E's on the eye chart opposite me sprang into
focus as crisp as new dollar bills.

The next week, he placed a pair of glasses on
the bridge of my nose and once more pressed the
lamp and his face next to my cheek. I could feel
the warm breath whistling through his nostrils,
saw the pores in his cheeks, the black stubble already beginning to shade his face. He reached
out his arms to help me down from the chair, and
as I turned dizzily in that room glittering with
glass cases and lenses and mirrors, I caught a
glimpse of the back of the white dress I had carefully chosen to wear for him. There, blossoming

like a poppy, was a bright red stain. There are so many ends to childhood. I count that day one of them.

I began to run. Had I bloodied the seat? Now I could never go back. Now I could never explain why I had kept the secret so long. Outside the world was fractured as sunlight bounced off my new lenses. My aunt had said to me once, "Can't your mother teach you how to comb your hair?" I tripped and went down on one knee. Girl with the crooked part: I hated myself.

"Wait, wait," the doctor shouted after me, but I yanked off the glasses and stumbled up my front steps. I didn't want to hear him tell me how soon I would not be able to see.

I COULD AFFORD TO TEACH IF I HAD A dollar for every person who has asked me if I really enjoy educating seventh- and eighth-graders. Adolescence is a twentieth-century invention most parents approach with dread and look back on with the relief of survivors. Why, then, would anyone willingly surround herself for nine months of the year with a gaggle of teen-agers? I can only tell you that the year I took a sabbatical from the small independent school where I have taught since 1974, I arranged to be out of the country when classes started in the fall. The ineluctable loss of mellow, apple-scented September mornings and my children, like their newly sharpened pencils, ready for the months ahead, was too much for me to bear.

May no one misunderstand me; I know my situation is a very special one. I teach at a private school of 190 students. We call eighteen children a large class. No security guards patrol our quiet corridors, no blizzard of paperwork engulfs our teachers, and except for the broadest of curriculum guides, we teach without hierarchical interference.

And teach we do. And more. There is a story to all this. Far back in my consciousness, in those shadowy places where memory sometimes blurs like watercolor on soft paper, an image keeps recurring to me. I see three young girls playing in a schoolyard. Perhaps this is recess on a late spring afternoon; surely it is hot. The defeated cotton of their plaid dresses seems to have long since forgotten the coolness of morning. Two of the girls dangle a heavy clothesline between them; each clasps a frayed end in one hand. Slowly, almost dreamily, they tease the rope back and forth, raising the playground dust in little coughs of smoke.

I am the third girl, of course, and not a part of them yet, my legs poised expectantly, one behind the other, elbows flexed like bird's wings. The girls toy with the rope a moment longer, and I wait. Their arms swing, at first in opposite directions, and the rope snakes, forms figure eights, is reluctant to leave the ground. Still I wait, and in a heartbeat more, their arms have found the order, the thick rope dances light, satisfying circles, and my head bobs in time to it all.

Now they wait for me, for I am timid, not yet certain of the beat, but suddenly I dare, and suddenly I am one with them, limp hair flying, legs gloriously skipping up and down, encircled by the steady rhythm of the rope and the twirling arms of my friends.

That scene is my emblem, the objective correlative for the kind of communion I believe successful teaching to be. Attention scatters in a classroom like papers dropped from a notebook. The bottled-up energy could move the Appalachians if it were harnessed. Frustration is there, and anger, and boredom ... satisfaction sometimes. Still there are days when all my energy and attention are channeled and my children and I are tuned into one another, and the current that flows between us could light up the world.

We are in seventh-grade English class working on vocabulary. I stand in the middle of my students. Such Mother Goose images come to my mind. I am a shepherdess; they are my lambs. I am a mother hen; they are my chicks. Solemnly I explain the importance of learning Greek and Latin roots. I speak test talk. I say, "E.R.B.,

S.A.T," tell them how to figure out meanings of words they aren't familiar with. Sitting in a room one day, far away from me, they will fill in grids, blacken in dots on answer sheets, and my remembered words will buoy them. I know it. I am the legendary schoolteacher. My students grow up to win Pulitzers, Nobel Peace Prizes, National Book Awards. While flashbulbs pop and microphones bristle, they honor me. "Yes," they say, "it was my seventh-grade English teacher. I owe it all to her."

But now we come to the end of the lesson, and I discover that half the children have failed to complete their homework. I have no patience for the excuses: the forgotten books, the papers left at home. What a transformation! I am the comic caricature of a schoolmarm. Who is flying around on her broomstick in here? I see myself as they must see me, my body elongated, hair drawn into a stingy knot, my needle nose an apt companion for the imaginary stick I carry. My voice echoes, nasal and strident in my own ears.

My students sit with their heads down, unable to look at me. Then, into the uncomfortable silence that follows, Bret crosses his muddy Nikes and says, "You've just delivered a tirade!" Well, there it is, a new vocabulary word, aptly used, and I can't resist countering with yet another word.

"At least your remark is pertinent," I tell him. Tension broken, voices rise. We are connected once more.

These twelve- and thirteen-year-olds come to me still filled with what Gerard Manley Hopkins calls "the dearest freshness deep down." I do not take my responsibilities lightly. This may well be the last time in their lives when they are absolutely open to the splendor of new impressions. Some have already been tarnished by negative experiences in the classroom. For them, the door has been slammed shut. I must put all the body English I possess behind my effort to pry open that door.

The first day of school, the children troop into the classroom, strangers to me and to one another. They stake out their territory, slump into desks, starting from the back of the room. Everyone keeps as far away from me and from the others as it is possible to be. When the room is quiet, they stare at me, their expressions as blank as the brand-new looseleaf binders in front of them. Now I am magician. It will be my joy and my goal to guide them gently into my circle, to take these green minds and, working with the alchemy of adolescence, transform them.

Teachers, like children, have a need for conviction and sustenance. There is a synergism that occurs when one mind respectfully encounters another. With good fortune, we can have it all: the steady rhythm of the rope and the encircling arms of friends.

AUNT ITKE, YOUR CHILDREN WRITE US
that they have admitted you to a nursing home.
As if we do not know the price of that decision,
they give excuses: you lost weight living alone,
forgot to take your medication, fell and fell again.
They say you are "better off" where you are now.
You will have proper meals and supervised activity. Nurses will monitor your health. You won't
turn the clock upside down, sleeping all day and
then wandering until first light.

But underneath the positive words of their letter, I hear uncertainty. "Better off" is a term they
have grappled with guiltily. Understand, we are
finally all such cowards in this business of what is
"best" for someone else. Most writers dodge the
issue, failing to document that age when, like
sleeves turned inside out, grown children become

parents of their parents and are forced to decisions that foreshadow their own fates.

The children say you ended up having a battle with your roommate the first night of your stay. You got up in the middle of the night and came back to the wrong bed. "Disoriented," they call it. But time collapses in the sleep and half-sleep of dream and demidream. Did you imagine you were in your childhood home again? Was it your sister, my mother, you reached for in the night? When you touched the sleeping body, age-dwarfed, curved like a question mark, was it her body you were seeking, her small waist to encircle, her sweet, shallow breathing to thaw your hands?

Aunt Itke, why do we wait so long to tell people we love them? Can you understand me now? I am a figure in the design of your memory—a leaf, a vine, a tender bud furled like a flag. Can you call me to your mind now? Do you remember who I am?

Aunt Itke, as I am a child still in you, so are you a young woman yet in me. I picture a torrid afternoon, half a century ago—a cool, dark room we called the "summer kitchen" and two sisters, one of them my mother, the other you. At an edge of the table where my mother sits, I pour sugar water from a toy teapot into small tin cups. You are everywhere: your fingers pluck a dead leaf from a trailing fern, lift the corner of a spotless dish towel draped on a down pillow of rising bread dough, fill a saucer of milk for the cats rubbing against your legs. And how you talk and laugh, the two of you, on and on through the summer hours, lulling me in the homeliness of your womanhood until my cheek rests on the table and I sleep.

I am mindful of the editing of innocence. We do not know what we cannot know. If you spoke then of empty pocketbooks and the monthly periods you cursed or prayed for, I was not aware of it. If your laughter was laced with irony when you joked about your husbands, what could I have known of that? Sickness, quarrels, accidents: the whirlwind of memory dies away, and what is left is the stillness of the Grecian urn.

My cousins write you are using a walker now. I find it hard to picture that. Somewhere you move with the grace that first named womanhood to me—from fern to rising bread to milk spilled in a saucer. Aunt Itke, hold on. Stay with us awhile; my childhood cradles in the shawl of your laughter.

FAR AHEAD OF US, PAST THE SIGN THAT reads "Emergency Entrance" and through the double doors, an orderly in a sea-green coat lounges behind a wheelchair and observes our slow progress. My mother-in-law is eighty years old. When she walks, her body lists from side to side like a wobbly table. I match my steps to her slow steps and wonder why the young man doesn't bring the wheelchair to help us. Struck by a whiplash of paranoia, I decide it has something to do with malpractice suits. After a while, I realize he probably doesn't see us at all.

Once inside, the injured old woman is safe for the moment in an armless chair. I look around at the reception room and at the long counter behind which several attractive young women laugh, chat, drink Tab from cans, and shuffle an occasional paper. Politely, I wait for one of them

143

to finish her conversation, and then I explain about my mother-in-law.

In the waiting room to my left a dozen men, women, and children of various ages and colors sit with the kind of resignation I remember from crowded bus stations during World War II. Which of us anticipated a trip to the emergency ward when we brushed our teeth this morning? Only an hour before, at noon, I had been finishing a brown-bag lunch, mentally marshaling my energies for that most challenging of arenas, a seventh-grade classroom on a Friday afternoon.

The telephone had interrupted my reverie. My son's voice at the other end, taut with the effort not to alarm me, described the fall his grandmother had taken. Selfishly, all I could think of was "broken hip," that trap that waits to be sprung in the lives of old people and those who care for them. A call to our doctor, a trip home to pick up my shaken mother-in-law, and here we are penciling in Social Security numbers and other vital statistics on hospital forms.

Now I hand back the papers as a wail of sirens foreshadows the arrival of fresh blood. One by one, five men and women in wheelchairs are brought in, a bizarre echo of Godard's movie *Weekend.* All victims of the same car crash, they sit with clipboards on their laps, their necks supported by identical rubber doughnuts. "Should have sent my kids to law school," I mutter through my teeth.

A young man wearing jeans and cowboy boots dumps his backpack on the floor and fills out forms. Around his head a rakish bandage winds, spotted with the color of dead roses. My mother-in-law sighs and says, "You could die here." For some reason, that remark cracks me up, but she doesn't get the joke. My Casio watch reads 2:34. Sadly, no human being with the exception of "In-take" has yet acknowledged our presence.

Our name is called. False alarm. I sign yet another paper and am told to have a seat. Longing to exert some control over the situation, I elect to stand. I am tempted to mention how long we *have* been sitting already, but I don't. I try not to look at my mother-in-law, who is obviously in pain. I wish I were more assertive. Why do I consider it un-American to make a scene? And if I did lose my temper, would they say, "This isn't my department," or "I'm on my lunch break," or "You'll have to speak to my supervisor?" If I asked, "Who's in charge?," would some ghost of Bud Abbot whisper, "He's on first?"

The man with the backpack pulls off his boots and stockings. Two potbellied children sidle up to one another, size each other up. "When did you have your kidney transplant?" a white-jacketed man asks the ashen-faced Indian across from us. A large black woman in a white knitted cap uses the bathroom. Two people make phone calls. My mother-in-law says, "Do something!" Her blue plaid wash dress is buttoned wrongly, and the sight of the crooked placket makes me want to weep. At 3:10 our name is called again. This time it's for real. I insist on a wheelchair and feel I have won a major victory when we get it.

My mother-in-law disappears behind a pair of double doors, but I am not allowed to go with her. A green jacket tells me brusquely, not unkindly, that I will be in the way back there. I scribble a shopping list on the back of an envelope and wait. Suddenly the backpacker pitches forward with his head between his legs. A woman who does not know him puts her arm around his shoulders. Someone yells in exasperation, "A man is passing out in here!" No one comes.

More sirens. A pink-coated attendant enters carrying something small and still, wrapped in a blanket. He walks slowly. The time for hurry seems to be over. I give the fainting man a cup of water. "Damn it," I say to no one in particular, "pay some attention here!" Marching to the desk, I point out the fainting man. "In-take" puts down her Tab and calls for a wheelchair. The backpacker is parked in a doorway where he can "get some air."

Five o'clock, and I screw up enough courage to ask "In-take" for news about my mother-in-law. Apologetically I say she has been inside two hours, she is old, she doesn't speak English too well. The five whiplash victims cradle their heads in their palms. The backpacker eats a package of tiny doughnuts from the vending machine. "Your mother will be OK," I am told. "It takes time."

Darkness outside. Red flashers project lurid stripes on the entry wall. "Heart attack," someone says. Flurry of activity. Uncertain again. Should I trouble them now? This is crazy. I take advantage of the temporarily opened door and sneak into the examining room. Alone, enclosed by a kind of white shower curtain, my mother-in-law lies on a plastic cot, a sheet wadded under her, hospital gown falling from her scrawny shoulder.

"Do something," she pleads. I look at her: pitiful remnant, once her family's protector and guide. Inside I say, "Ma, Ma, Ma." Now I am protector and guide in this topsy-turvy world where mothers turn into children and flesh reverses itself, falls away from the bone.

I grab the first uniformed person I can find—

147

an intern. He shakes off my hand and says sharply, "Can't you see people are dying here?" I've had it. And I say so. The intern's lower eyelids looked rimmed in blood. He is angry with me. He calls me "lady," and wonders where I've been lately. Hugging his clipboard, he leans against a doorjamb. He is a bottle, unstoppered. Don't I read the newspapers? They are shorthanded; their funds have been cut.

But now I'm angry too. I've heard these excuses before, at the end of phone lines, from behind wire cages. Their cost is too dear. I tell the young intern I believe people should not be forced to trade their humanity for needed services. A pat on the back or a word of assurance do not cost money. And then I remember Emily's scalding lesson in *Our Town*. "We don't have time to look at one another," I say. The intern takes off his glasses and rubs the bridge of his nose with thumb and forefinger, but I am not finished. "Times are not getting any better," I tell him. "We may all have to depend, one day, on the kindness of strangers."

Seven-thirty. We go through the sliding doors. The intern wheels my mother-in-law's chair. Even though he is off duty now, he has offered to do this for us. Together we get her into my car, protecting the bandaged shoulder. I can't believe how touched I am by his considerateness. I wave to him through the car window. I want to say thank you to him for remembering we are human beings, but then, on second thought, perhaps he should say thank you to us—for reminding him.

Flannery O'Connor has a wonderful short story, "A Temple of the Holy
Ghost," in which the protagonist, a child of
twelve, hears about the half-man, half-woman at
the county fair and cannot understand how such
a creature can exist if it doesn't have two heads.
My seventh-graders thought the child woefully
immature and spoke about the "old days" when
parents didn't talk to children about such things.
One of their classmates proceeded to speak so
knowledgeably about hermaphrodites and sex-
change operations that my head swam.

Orchestrating the discussion that followed was
not a simple task. I wanted to answer questions
honestly, yet was concerned about raising alarm
in children preoccupied with their own emerging
sexuality. I thought about the student a few years
back who began her first menstrual period in

school. "I know all about it," she said, impatiently, when I tried to help her. "I just forgot to find out how you stop it when you have to go to school."

Seventh grade is such a catchall of contrasts. There are girls with bodies as flat as yardsticks and others whose curves cause near collisions on Connecticut Avenue at lunchtime. Boys with baby fat and sweet sopranos play soccer with classmates who already flutter the hearts of "older women."

Miss O'Connor's story describes that area of childhood that laps over onto the bank of adolescence. I found myself picking my way ever so tentatively in a classroom where children of roughly the same age could be on opposite shores of sexual awareness. Even though all considered themselves well informed, I could see by their puzzled faces how confused they really were.

Because of a combination of factors, both physical and social, children enter adolescence, or assume the attributes of it, earlier and earlier. There are days I wish I could hold back the clock for some of my students. Donning a pair of Calvins isn't a ticket to the adult world, nor does a sex-education lecture guarantee safe passage. Even with Judy Blume to hold their hands, life for most young teenagers is as complicated as the

Rubik's Cube. Even their own native language betrays them sometimes.

Whenever I read "The Raven" to my class, I lose a couple of the boys as soon as I reach the lines about "The dusty bust of Pallas." Lord alone knows what erotic picture that image evokes, but the squirming bodies and flushed faces tell me I have hit a nerve every time. "Get ahold of yourselves," I say, and everyone laughs, and two-thirds of the kids spend the rest of the class worrying because they didn't get the joke.

I watch the groups forming at the beginning of the school year, see the boys on one side of the room, jostling one another, unaware mostly of the power they will soon sense, but not soon understand. At the other side cluster the girls, some still in braids, the blood already singing in their veins. In a few weeks, the more socially precocious boys and girls will have paired off; most of the rest will be wishing they could. Only a few stragglers will remain oblivious of the old ritual.

The stragglers interest me, for as inevitably as sunrise I know I will be witness to their awakening. Like sunflowers they grow, almost before my eyes, noses losing their anonymity, bodies elongating, arms and legs seemingly having a life of their own. One day, who knows by what alchemy, they are on the other side, and the relief they feel at having made the leap is almost palpable. They signal us all, sprawling at their desks on the backs of their necks, skinny blue-jeaned legs all over the aisle ways.

I hadn't been through *Tom Sawyer* for years until I read it with my seventh grade this fall. Comparison is one of the compasses by which we chart our lives, and I couldn't help seeing how differently from me my students reacted to the story. They were sophisticated enough to brand "dainty" Becky and "boisterous" Tom as products of Twain's sexism, but they readily conceded that Tom enjoys more freedom than they do. No sneaking out of the house at midnight or, as one student wrote, playing "hockey" from school, for them. Fear of mothers and the truant officer takes care of those romantic notions. Besides, they say, not without some satisfaction, parental reprisal would be swift and sure.

Young adolescents are painfully aware of their conflicts with parents. Most see these battles as a necessary part of growing up. "Parents say that when you're a teenager, you talk back," one of my students told me, "but that's because now that you're older, you have more of an opinion on things."

"When you are little," another added, "parents give you a one-sided story and you believe it.

Getting older means learning there is another side and having doubts."

Small wonder these children speak of doubts. In this Alice-in-Wonderland world, some girls have to compete with their mothers for a corner of the looking glass, as both find themselves preening for a date on the same evening. One thirteen-year-old boy I recently taught sat in my office and wept because his father insisted on how much they had in common now that he was divorced. "He keeps trying to get me to talk about problems I have with girls," the boy said, "but all the time I'm worrying whether *he's* making it or not."

Even housing becomes a kind of Virginia reel for many children I know. Joint custody can mean four days in one house with mother and her new family and three days in another with father and a different brood. Kids used to say, "I haven't got my homework because my dog chewed it up." Now they tell me, "I left it at my dad's." With so many new configurations of personalities to deal with, where is the time for Longfellow's "long long thoughts" of youth?

But thanks to those very parents with whom they have conflicts, my students, for all their insecurities about changing bodies and growing sexual awareness, are more comfortable in their sexuality than my generation ever was. I pieced together the menstrual cycle from whispers and discarded bloody rags. Every boy and girl in my seventh grade knows more about the "facts of life" than my mother did after having four children.

Yes, the world in which *we* grew up is different from the one our children inhabit, but some things are eternal. Children teetering on the cusp of maturity will always be drawn by the sense of a secret on the other side. In that crossing, we, as parents and teachers, stand in the relationship of map to the reality of land. Our children must trust our guideposts, while we must pray that we point them in the right direction. For though they travel in unfamiliar lands, if they follow our signs correctly, they will find their way home again to us, someday.

SHE SAT, HIDDEN FROM ME BY THE BACK
of her great wing chair. In front of her a black
and white TV set flickered a battle between the
Orioles and the Yankees. I thought, How small
she has become, shrinking like Alice, over the
years.

Her right arm in a sling hugged her side; the
left lay in her lap, curled and trembling. She had
dozed off waiting for the evening news, and when
I touched her arm, her startled pupils behind the
thick lenses looked large as blueberries.

It was my job to "bell the cat," frivolous as
that may have sounded. I had rehearsed my
speech so many times; now I wanted only to get
it over with. "Ma," I blurted, raising my voice,
"you know Jack and I are supposed to go away
next week?" She nodded, apprehensively.
"Well," we can't leave you alone with that bro-

ken arm." Her left hand began to shake even more violently than before. "Unfair," I whispered, tempted to get out of the room quickly and forget the whole thing.

"No, you can't let her win this one," I said to myself, disgusted with my choice of verbs. Where was the contest here, and who were the antagonists? Our family was caught in a situation that was a mere preview of coming attractions. If our plan was to keep her living at home with us, we *had* to have an occasional break, or we would end up killing one another.

"Ma," I persisted, "we have found out a wonderful thing." I tried to make my voice sound casual. "The Hebrew Home has a program for people like us who have their parents living with them. They will take care of you for a few days while we're gone."

My mother-in-law stared into the TV screen as if the great questions of the universe were answered there. In Yankee Stadium someone lay down a perfect sacrifice bunt, sending his teammate to second base safely. "Do you hear me?" I asked, pulling at the sleeve of her good arm. "Aren't we lucky to have such a place for you to be safe while we're away?"

Still she stared without speaking, and self-righteous anger traded places with my guilt.

Weren't we entitled to some worry-free time? Hadn't we cared for her for many years? I hugged myself with crossed arms as if it were winter instead of July. "Answer me this," I shouted, "can you stay by yourself with that arm?"

"No," she admitted, clearing her throat.

"Then what's wrong, for heaven's sake?"

She turned the blueberry irises toward me then and said quietly, almost shamefacedly, "They put my mother in an old folks' home, and she never came back." I walked out of the room and told my husband it was his problem; I didn't have the guts to push the issue any further.

Days passed. My husband and I whispered together in our room at night. He issued ultimatums, his voice rising. Either she agreed to go to temporary care or he would pack her off to the Hebrew Home for good. "Shh," I cautioned. "She'll hear you." "Good! Let her hear." But he lowered his voice all the same.

I tried to puzzle out who had rights in this throwback of a family. Having lived with grandparents ourselves, where had we ever found the *chutzpah* to think we could do better than our parents? My mother used to complain endlessly about my grandfather. The smoldering Luckies he left everywhere convinced her we would all be consumed in a fire started by the one smoking butt she failed to find and stub out. Years ago, I had seen my mother-in-law turn on her own mother in a fury when the old woman criticized her housekeeping once too often.

None of our friends seemed to have the extended-family problem. Their parents conveniently lived on the West Coast or in Florida or Arizona, places from which they were always taking lengthy trips to exotic destinations. These parents visited their children twice a year and brought *presents.*

Meanwhile, the telephone jangled constantly, like the background noise for a police-station series on TV. Each of our four children called daily for bulletins. They stood behind us, they said, but I felt their ambivalence. On the one hand, they reassured us. "Go, you deserve it." In another way, they seemed to be judging us. It was easy for them, I thought, now that they could look at their grandmother from the nostalgic distance of their own homes.

At breakfast, cutting my mother-in-law's food into bite-sized pieces, I imagined the years passing, the three of us growing older together. In my most self-pitying projections, we all entered the Hebrew Home for the Aged at one time, each bent over an identical aluminum walker. In the end I decided I was no Christian martyr despite what our friends said, so early one afternoon, I tried again.

This time my mother-in-law was watching Donahue. I turned down the volume and plunged right in. The shrunken body and shaking hand were not going to divert me today, I vowed. "Ma," I said, "do you know what the Jewish Torah is?"

"What did you say?" she asked suspiciously. I repeated my question. "Of course I know what the Jewish Torah is!"

"OK. Which hand am I holding up?"

"Your right one," she said, after a moment.

"Look at me, Ma." (I couldn't believe I was doing this.) Slowly and clearly I said, "I swear on the Jewish Torah, I will go and pick you up and bring you home the minute I get off the airplane." I paused for dramatic effect. "Now do you believe me?" The old woman turned to the screen again. Then, looking back at me, she shrugged her shoulders and turned her palms out in her lap as if to say, "What difference does it make?"

I could feel the onset of a monumental hot flash, but I wouldn't let go. "OK," I said, grinding my teeth. "You knew my mother, right?" She nodded, once more. "I loved my mother, didn't I?" I didn't wait for a reply. Almost shouting now, I said, "I swear on my mother's memory that I will not leave you in that home!"

My mother-in-law picked up a bottle from the table where the TV stood. "The aspirin doesn't help the pain anymore," she said, not looking at me.

Shaking, I walked out of her room and slammed the door. Molly Picon couldn't have given a better performance on the Jewish stage, I told myself, but this wasn't funny. I was shattered. I knew that no principle and certainly no mere vacation was worth this kind of emotional vein stripping.

Standing with my back to the bedroom door, I heard the telephone dial slowly clicking forward and back. "Lizzy," my mother-in-law said to my daughter (and her voice was strong), "did you hear? Mama and Daddy are going for vacation." A pause, and then, "I'll go myself a few days to the Hebrew Home. You know I can't stay alone with my broken arm." I put my hand over my eyes. "Bring your spoons, Lizzy," she continued. "When I come home, I'll polish them for you."

ABOUT THE AUTHOR

Faye Moskowitz is a guest commentator for "All Things Considered" and a contributor to *The Washington Post* and to *The New York Times* "Hers" column, where several of the essays in this book had their beginnings. She lives in Washington, D.C., with her husband, has four grown children, and is a director of and teacher at The Edmund Burke School there.

A LEAK IN THE HEART

was set in Electra on the Americomp system by
American–Stratford Graphic Services, Inc., Brattle-
boro, Vermont. Designed originally as a linotype face
by William Addison Dwiggins for the Mergenthaler
Linotype Company and first made available in 1935,
Electra is impossible to classify as either "modern" or
"old-style." Not based on any historical model or reflecting any particular period or style, it is notable for
its clean and elegant lines, its lack of contrast between
thick and thin elements that characterize most modern faces, and its freedom from all idiosyncracies
that catch the eye and interfere with reading.

A LEAK IN THE HEART was printed and bound by
Maple-Vail Book Manufacturing Group,
Binghamton, New York.

Designed by Anne Chalmers.